Patrice-Anne Rutledge

Sams **Teach Yourself**

Google™+

in **10 Minutes**

SAMS | 800 East 96th Street, Indianapolis, Indiana 46240

Sams Teach Yourself Google™+ in 10 Minutes, Second Edition

ISBN-13: 978-0-672-33613-3
ISBN-10: 0-672-33613-8

Library of Congress Cataloging-in-Publication

Rutledge, Patrice-Anne.
  Sams teach yourself Google+ in 10 minutes / Patrice-Anne Rutledge. — 2nd ed.
       p. cm. — (Sams teach yourself)
  ISBN 978-0-672-33613-3
  1. Google+ (Electronic resource) 2. Online social networks.
3. Social networks—Computer network resources. I. Title. II.
Title: Sams teach yourself Google plus in ten minutes.
  HM743.G66.R88 2012
  006.7'54—dc23

                                                            2012017128

Printed in the United States of America

First Printing June 2012

Trademarks

All terms mentioned in this book that are known to be trademarks or service marks have been appropriately capitalized. Pearson Education, Inc. cannot attest to the accuracy of this information. Use of a term in this book should not be regarded as affecting the validity of any trademark or service mark.

Warning and Disclaimer

Every effort has been made to make this book as complete and as accurate as possible, but no warranty or fitness is implied. The information provided is on an "as is" basis. The author and the publisher shall have neither liability nor responsibility to any person or entity with respect to any loss or damages arising from the information contained in this book.

Bulk Sales

Pearson Education, Inc. offers excellent discounts on this book when ordered in quantity for bulk purchases or special sales. For more information, please contact

U.S. Corporate and Government Sales
1-800-382-3419
corpsales@pearsontechgroup.com

For sales outside of the U.S., please contact

International Sales
international@pearson.com

Editor-in-Chief
Greg Wiegand

Executive Editor
Rick Kughen

Managing Editor
Kristy Hart

Project Editor
Anne Goebel

Copyeditor
Barbara Hacha

Indexer
Lisa Stumpf

Proofreader
Debbie Williams

Publishing Coordinator
Cindy Teeters

Book Designer
Gary Adair

Compositor
Nonie Ratcliff

Contents

Introduction   **1**

1 **Introducing Google+**   **3**

Exploring Google+ 3

Signing Up for Google+ 5

Signing In to Google+ 12

Navigating Google+ 13

Accessing Popular Google+ Features 14

Getting Help 15

Sending Feedback 16

Summary 17

2 **Working with Google+ Profiles**   **19**

Understanding Google+ Profiles 19

Adding a Profile Cover Photo 21

     Adding a Single Cover Photo 21

     Adding a Photo Scrapbook to Your Profile 23

     Deleting a Photo 25

Changing Your Profile Photo 26

     Editing Your Name 26

Editing Your Profile's About Tab 27

     Specifying Profile Privacy by Section 30

     Adding Links on Your Google+ Profile 32

Specifying Your Contact Settings 36

Specifying the People to Display on Your Profile 37

     Viewing Your Profile as Others See It 39

Adding a Google+ Profile Button to Your Website 40

Summary 40

3 Creating a Google+ Page for Your Business   41

Understanding Google+ Pages Versus Google+ Profiles 41

Creating a Google+ Page 42

Using Google+ as a Page 48

Managing Your Google+ Page Settings 49

  Specifying Who Can Interact with You and Your Posts 50

  Specifying Your Notification Delivery Preferences 50

  Managing Your Email Subscriptions 50

  Specifying Notification Preferences 50

  Customizing Your Circles 51

  Managing Photo Settings 51

  Deleting a Google+ Page 51

Adding Google+ Page Managers 52

  Removing a Google+ Manager 53

  Transferring Ownership of a Google+ Page 54

Summary 55

4 Managing Your Network with Circles   57

Understanding Google+ Circles 57

Creating New Circles 59

Adding People to Circles 60

  Adding People to Circles from the Find People Tab 61

  Adding Your Email Contacts 63

  Adding People and Pages that Google+ Suggests 66

  Adding People from the Notifications Menu 66

  Adding People from Their Google+ Profile 68

Managing Circles 69

  Viewing People in Your Circles 69

  Viewing People Who Added You to Their Circles 69

  Moving People from One Circle to Another 70

Removing People from Circles 71

Editing a Circle's Name and Description 71

Deleting a Circle 72

Sharing a Circle 72

Summary 74

5 **Managing Google+ Settings and Privacy**   **75**

Understanding Google+ Privacy 75

Managing Your Google Account Settings 75

Deleting Your Google+ Profile 77

Deleting Your Google Account 78

Managing Your Security 79

Managing Your Privacy Settings 80

Managing Privacy Settings for Your Google+ Profile 81

Managing Google+ Sharing 81

Managing Other Google+ Privacy Options 82

Managing Google+ Settings 83

Specifying Who Can Interact with You and Your Posts 83

Setting Notification Delivery Preferences 84

Managing Email Subscriptions 84

Specifying Notification Preferences 85

Enabling +1 Personalization 86

Adding Google+ Pages to Your Circles 86

Displaying Content About Google+ Games 87

Customizing Your Circles 87

Managing Google+ Photo Settings 87

Managing Your Products 87

Specifying Your Preferred Languages 88

Backing Up Your Data 89

Summary 91

6 **Sharing Content on Google+**   **93**

Using the Share Box 93

    Formatting Your Posts 98

    Mentioning Other People in Your Posts 99

Sharing Photos 100

Sharing Videos 103

Sharing Links 105

Summary 107

7 **Viewing Your Google+ Stream**   **109**

Exploring Your Stream 109

    Accessing Your Stream 110

    Viewing a Sample Post 110

    Filtering Your Stream 113

Participating in the Stream 114

    Liking a Post Using the +1 Button 114

    Commenting on Posts 116

    Sharing Posts 117

Managing Your Posts in the Stream 120

    Editing a Post 121

    Deleting a Post 122

    Disabling Comments 122

    Locking a Post 123

    Reporting or Deleting Comments 123

Managing Your Circles' Posts in the Stream 125

    Linking to a Post 125

    Reporting Abuse 126

    Muting a Post 127

    Viewing the Explore Page 128

Summary 129

8 Searching on Google+   **131**

Searching Google+ Content 131

Filtering Google+ Search Results 133

Saving a Google+ Search 133

Summary 134

9 Viewing and Managing Notifications   **135**

Understanding Google+ Notifications 135

Viewing Your Notifications on Google+ 136

Viewing the Notifications Page 139

Receiving Notifications via Email and Text Message 140

Specifying Who Can Send You Notifications 141

Summary 141

10 Working with Photos   **143**

Exploring Google+ Photo Options 143

Uploading Photos to Google+ 143

Exploring the Photos Page 144

Creating and Managing Photo Albums 145

Creating a Photo Album 146

Viewing Your Photo Albums 147

Sharing an Album 148

Updating Album Sharing Settings 150

Organizing an Album 151

Deleting an Album 152

Adding Photos to an Existing Album 153

Working in the Photo Lightbox 154

Exploring the Lightbox 155

Tagging Photos 156

Editing Photos Using Creative Kit 161

Summary 162

11 **Chatting on Google+**   **163**

Understanding Google+ Chat 163

Exploring the Chat List 163

Specifying Your Chat Availability 164

Specifying Your Chat Privacy Settings 165

Chatting on Google+ 166

Participating in a Chat 166

Sending a File 169

Using Voice and Video Chat 170

Chatting Off the Record 174

Signing Out of Chat 176

Summary 176

12 **Using Hangouts for Video Chat**   **177**

Understanding Hangouts 177

Preparing to Use Hangouts 177

Viewing the Hangouts Page 178

Starting a Hangout 178

Inviting People to a Hangout 184

Joining a Hangout 184

Adding Group Text Chat to a Hangout 186

Adding Apps to Your Hangouts 188

Using Screenshare During a Hangout 188

Adding YouTube Video to Your Hangout 189

Applying Google Effects to Your Hangout 191

Using Google Docs During a Hangout 191

Adding Other Apps 191

Muting During a Hangout 191

Ending a Hangout 192

Summary 192

13 **Playing Games**   **193**

Exploring Google+ Games 193

Playing a Game 193

Summary 198

14 **Using Google+ Mobile**   **199**

Exploring Google+ Mobile 199

Using the Google+ Android App 200

Using the Google+ iPhone App 201

Using the Google+ Mobile Web App 203

Using the Google+ Mobile Basic Web App 203

Summary 204

Index   **205**

About the Author

Patrice-Anne Rutledge is a business technology author and journalist specializing in social media, online applications, and small business technology. Her other books include *Sams Teach Yourself LinkedIn in 10 Minutes*, *Using LinkedIn*, *Using Facebook*, and *The Truth About Profiting from Social Networking*, all from Pearson. Through Rutledge Communications, she also offers writing and editing services to businesses and nonprofits worldwide. You can reach Patrice through her website at www.patricerutledge.com.

Dedication

To my family, with thanks for their ongoing support and encouragement.

Acknowledgments

Special thanks to Rick Kughen, Anne Goebel, and Barbara Hacha for their feedback, suggestions, and attention to detail.

We Want to Hear from You!

As the reader of this book, you are our most important critic and commentator. We value your opinion and want to know what we're doing right, what we could do better, what areas you'd like to see us publish in, and any other words of wisdom you're willing to pass our way.

We welcome your comments. You can email or write directly to let us know what you did or didn't like about this book—as well as what we can do to make our books stronger.

Please note that we cannot help you with technical problems related to the topic of this book.

When you write, please be sure to include this book's title and author as well as your name and phone or email address. We will carefully review your comments and share them with the author and editors who worked on the book.

E-mail: consumer@samspublishing.com

Mail: Sams Publishing
          ATTN: Reader Feedback
          800 East 96th Street
          Indianapolis, IN 46240 USA

Reader Services

Visit our website and register this book at informit.com/register for convenient access to any updates, downloads, or errata that might be available for this book.

Introduction

Google+ is Google's answer to social sharing on the Web. Soon after its launch of a limited field trial on June 28, 2011, Google+ already had tens of millions of members; thousands more joined every day, eagerly seeking out invitations from friends and colleagues. When Google+ opened to the public in mid-September 2011, its user base jumped more than 30 percent within days.

If you use other social sites, such as Facebook, LinkedIn, or Twitter, the basic concepts of Google+ should seem familiar to you. You can post text-based updates, photos, videos, and links; comment on posts from people you know and follow; share interesting content from around the Web; and much more. Google+ has several unique features as well, such as the power to maintain complete control over how you share each piece of content you post. Google+ also extends beyond traditional social networking to offer unlimited uploading and storage of photos and videos, video chats, group text messaging, and more.

Sams Teach Yourself Google+ in 10 Minutes, Second Edition is designed to get you up and running on Google+ as quickly as possible. Because Google+ is still under development and its functionality will continue to change over time, the features available may vary at any given time. The companion website to this book will help keep you updated on what's new with Google+. For now, turn to Lesson 1, "Introducing Google+," to get started with this powerful social-sharing tool.

Who Is This Book For?

This book is for you if...

▶ You're new to Google+ and want to learn what it's all about.

▶ You want to share content, photos, and videos on the Web with friends, family, and colleagues, and you've heard that Google+ is a great way to do this.

▶ You want to become productive on Google+ as quickly as possible and are short on time.

Companion Website

This book has a companion website online at www.patricerutledge.com/books/google-plus.

Visit the site to access the following:

▶ Book updates

▶ News about Google+ enhancements and features

▶ Other books and articles that may be of interest to you

Conventions Used in This Book

The Teach Yourself series has several unique elements that will help you as you are learning more about Google+. These include the following:

> NOTE: A note presents interesting pieces of information related to the surrounding discussion.

> TIP: A tip offers advice or teaches an easier way to do something.

> CAUTION: A caution advises you about potential problems and helps you steer clear of disaster.

> PLAIN ENGLISH: Plain English icons provide clear definitions of new, essential terms.

LESSON 1

Introducing Google+

In this lesson, you explore Google+ and learn how to set up your Google+ account.

Exploring Google+

Google+ is Google's social networking site that emphasizes real-life sharing where you're in control of exactly who sees—or doesn't see—your content. Launched on June 28, 2011, Google+ has tens of millions of users, with thousands of new users joining every day.

In addition to its extensive social sharing features, Google+ also enables you to chat with friends via text and video, upload unlimited photos and videos, play games, and more. Google+ integrates automatically with other Google applications you may already use, including Profiles, Picasa, Gmail, and more.

If you use other social sites such as Facebook, LinkedIn, or Twitter, the basic concepts of Google+ should be familiar to you. Google+ has several unique features, however, and its own terminology. You'll learn more about each of these features as you read through this book, but for now, it's a good idea to become familiar with these Google+ terms:

▶ **Profile.** Your profile is your public presence on Google+ that includes your photo, information about your background, and links to your other sites on the Web. You can create a Google+ profile only for an individual. If you use Facebook or LinkedIn, the concept of a profile should be familiar to you. With Google+, you have control over each section on your profile and can specify exactly who can see that section. For example, you can display a detailed profile to people you know and reveal less

information to those you don't. To view a sample Google+
profile, visit my profile at https://plus.google.com/
108294135476012165013.

> NOTE: **How Can I Shorten My Google+ Profile URL?**
> By default, your Google+ profile URL includes a 21-digit identifier.
> Google+ doesn't offer custom URLs at this time, but you can use a
> third-party tool, such as gplus.to (http://gplus.to) or Plusya (http://
> plusya.com), to create a custom URL. For example, my Google+ pro-
> file shortened with gplus.to is http://gplus.to/PatriceRutledge.

▶ **Page.** A Google+ page enables a business, brand, or organization
to have a professional presence on Google+. If you're familiar
with Facebook pages, the functionality of Google+ pages should
be familiar to you. To view a sample Google+ page, visit
Google's official Google+ page at https://plus.google.com/
116899029375914044550.

▶ **Circles.** Circles enable you to organize your Google+ network by
placing people into distinct groups, such as Family, Friends, and
Acquaintances. When you post content on Google+, you can
specify exactly which circles can view each post. You can also
specify privacy settings by circle. This gives you complete control over who sees what content. Placing people in a Google+ circle is similar to following people on Twitter. They don't need to
accept a formal request and can choose whether they want to
place you in one of their circles (in other words, whether they
want to follow you back).

▶ **Stream.** The Google+ stream offers a central location for viewing the posts, links, photos, and videos that you and others have
shared. You can join the conversation on the stream by adding
your own posts and comments, sharing interesting content you
discover, and supporting quality posts using the Google +1 button. If you're familiar with Facebook, the Google+ stream is similar to the Facebook Wall but with added privacy controls.

▶ **+1 button.** The Google +1 button offers a way to publicly show
your support for a post that you like. The +1 button is available

on Google+ and, optionally, on other websites and blogs that choose to enable this button. Google+ uses the term "+1" as both a noun and a verb. Using Google+ terminology, you +1 a post using the +1 button. In many ways, the +1 button is similar to the Like button on Facebook.

▶ **Hangouts.** Hangouts enable you to get together with other Google+ users using live video chat. You can even watch a YouTube video together during a hangout. In addition to regular hangouts, Google+ also offers Hangouts with Extras and Hangouts On Air, which enable you to collaborate with others in real-time and reach a wider audience.

▶ **Messenger.** Participate in group texting, either one-on-one or with the people in one of your Google+ circles. You can invite others or receive a notification on your status bar when someone invites you. This feature is currently available only for the Google+ Android app and Google+ iPhone app.

▶ **Instant Upload.** Upload photos and videos automatically from your Android 2.1+ smartphone or iPhone to a private Google+ album. You can later make any photos or videos public if you choose to share them.

Signing Up for Google+

Google+ requires you to have an existing Google account. If you already use another Google product—such as Gmail, AdWords, or Reader—you have a Google account. For example, you can use your Gmail address to sign up for Google+. If you don't have a Google account, you can sign up for one when you sign up for Google+. In addition, you must be at least 18 years old to participate on Google+.

NOTE: **How Does Google+ Work with Google Apps?**
Companies that use Google Apps can manually enable Google+ for their users. If your company has enabled this feature, you can sign up for a Google+ profile at www.google.com/+ just like anyone else with a Google account.

To sign up for Google+, follow these steps:

1. Navigate to www.google.com/+, as shown in Figure 1.1.

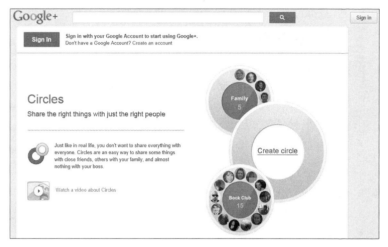

FIGURE 1.1 Signing up for Google+ takes just a few minutes.

2. If you aren't signed in to your Google account, click the **Sign In** button to open Google's sign-in page. Enter your email and password and click the **Sign In** button. If you are signed in to your Google account, you don't need to sign in again.

NOTE: **How Do I Sign Up for a Google Account?**

If you don't have an existing Google account, click the **Create an Account** link on the Google+ page. The Create an Account page opens, where you can sign up for a Google account. When you're done, return to the Google+ page to sign up for Google+.

---

3. Verify that your first and last names are correct on the Google+ sign-up page, shown in Figure 1.2. By default, Google+ uses the First Name and Last Name fields from your Google account.

FIGURE 1.2 Google+ connects with your existing Google account.

TIP: **You Can Also Sign Up for Google+ by Responding to an Invitation**

If a friend invites you to Google+, you'll receive your invitation by email. Click the **Join Google+** button in the email you receive. If your email address is associated with a Google account, the Google+ sign-up page displays (refer to Figure 1.2). If Google doesn't recognize your email address, you're prompted to sign in to your Google account or create a new account.

CAUTION: **You Must Use Your Real Name on Google+**

Google+ requires that you use your real name when creating a Google+ profile. If you have privacy concerns, you can specify exactly who has access to the information you post on Google+. To learn more about the Google+ name policy and its exceptions, visit http://support.google.com/plus/bin/answer.py?hl=en&answer=1228271.

4. Select your **Gender** from the drop-down list.

5. Click the **Add Your Photo** link to open the Select Profile Photo dialog box, shown in Figure 1.3.

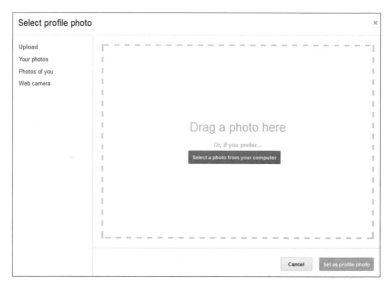

Select profile photo   ×

Upload
Your photos
Photos of you
Web camera

Drag a photo here

Or, if you prefer...

Select a photo from your computer

Cancel   Set as profile photo

FIGURE 1.3   Select a photo to display on your Google+ profile.

TIP: **Add a Photo Using Drag and Drop**

Optionally, you can drag and drop a photo to the Select Profile Photo dialog box. For example, if you have Windows Explorer open in a separate, minimized window, you can select your photo and drag it to this dialog box.

---

6. Click the **Select a Photo from Your Computer** button.

7. In the File Upload dialog box, select the photo you want to upload and click the **Open** button. Depending on your browser and operating system, this dialog box and button could have different names.

8. In the Select Profile Photo dialog box, shown in Figure 1.4, drag the four white squares that surround your photo to crop it to the desired size.

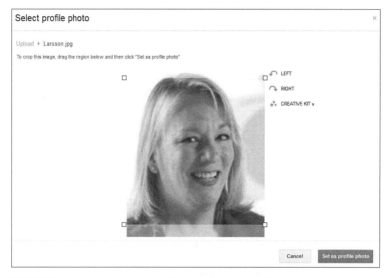

FIGURE 1.4   Crop your photo to fit in the space provided.

TIP: **Quickly Fix Problems with Your Photo**
Optionally, you can click the **Left** or **Right** button next to your photo to fix rotation problems. If you need to fix cosmetic issues such as red eye or color contrast, click the **Creative Kit** button to open Picnik (www.picnik.com), a web-based photo-editing application where you can enhance your photo.

9. Click the **Set as Profile Photo** button. Google+ returns to the sign-up box where your photo now displays (see Figure 1.5).

10. By default, Google uses your information to personalize content and ads on non-Google websites. If you don't want Google to use your Google+ data to personalize ads in this manner, remove the check mark from the check box that displays below your photo.

11. Click the **Upgrade** button in the lower-right corner of the page to join Google+.

FIGURE 1.5   Return to the sign-up page to finish the sign-up process.

12. Optionally, you can search for your email contacts on sites such as Yahoo! or Hotmail. In general, however, it's a good idea to complete your profile first before connecting with others. Click the **Continue** button to skip this step for now.

13. Google+ prompts you to add people to circles, suggesting several people you might know, based on your email address. You can add people to circles now or add them later. In general, it's a good idea to understand how circles work and affect your privacy before adding a lot of people to circles. See Lesson 4, "Managing Your Network with Circles," for more information. Click the **Continue** button to go to the next step.

14. Google+ prompts you to add some well-known people and celebrities to your circles. Again, you can do this now or wait until you've learned more about circles. If you want to add people now, it's recommended to add celebrities to your Following circle because you don't actually know them. Click the **Continue** button to go to the next step.

15. Google+ prompts you to enter basic profile data, such as the school you attended, your employer, and the places you lived

(see Figure 1.6). When you start typing the name of a school or
employer, Google+ displays a drop-down list of potential
matches for you to choose from. Although entering this data is
optional, it makes it easier for the people you know to find you.

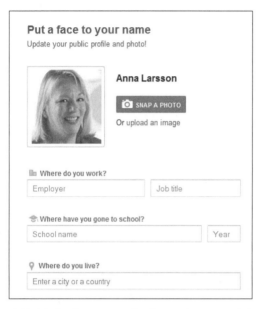

FIGURE 1.6   Add details about your schools, employers, and places you've
lived.

NOTE: **You Can Expand Your Profile After Signing Up for
Google+**
Google+ asks you to enter basic profile data during the sign-up
process, but you can expand your profile later, even specifying
exactly who can see each section of your profile. See Lesson 2,
"Working with Google+ Profiles," for more information.

16. Click the **Upload an Image** link if you want to change the profile photo you uploaded. Optionally, you can click the **Snap a
Photo** button to a take a picture with your webcam. If you're satisfied with your profile photo, you can skip this step.

17. Click the **Finish** button in the lower-right corner of the screen.

Google+ opens, displaying your stream (see Figure 1.7).

FIGURE 1.7   Your stream displays posts from people in your circles.

Your stream displays the posts of the people you added to circles during steps 12, 13, and 14 as well as Hot on Google+ posts from people not in your circles that Google+ deems particularly interesting or informative. If you haven't added anyone yet, your stream displays only Hot on Google+ posts—for now. In Lesson 7, "Viewing Your Google+ Stream," you learn how to customize the number of Hot on Google+ posts that display on your stream.

From here, you can complete your profile, add people to circles, specify your privacy settings, and then start participating on Google+ by adding your own content and commentary.

Signing In to Google+

After you have a Google+ account, you can sign in by going to the Google+ website (www.google.com/+/), clicking the **Sign In** button, and entering your email address and password (refer to Figure 1.1).

If you're already signed in to another Google application (such as Gmail), click your first name in the upper-left corner of the Google bar to open Google+ (see Figure 1.8). Be aware that you must have signed up for Google+ for this link to be available.

FIGURE 1.8   You can also access Google+ from the Google bar.

Navigating Google+

The left side of Google+ displays a navigation ribbon that enables you to access popular Google+ features easily (see Figure 1.9).

FIGURE 1.9   Quickly find the content and features you want using the Google+ navigation ribbon.

The ribbon includes the following icons: Home, Profile, Explore, Hangouts, Photos, Circles, Games, Pages, and More. Because the ribbon is dynamic, the order in which the icons display varies and not all icons display at the same time. (Some are hidden in the More pop-out menu.) You can use your mouse to drag and drop icons so that those you use the most are on the top. The only icons you can't move are Home and More (but you can change the icons that display in More).

If you don't use a particular icon very often, you can drop it on the More icon where it stays hidden from view until you need it. For example, if you don't have a page or don't play games often, you could move those icons to More.

To access related features, pause your mouse over an icon to display a menu of options (not all icons have this feature yet). For example, when you pause your mouse over the Photos icon, you can choose to add photos, view photos from your phone, or view your photo albums. When you pause over the More icon, you can view the icons you've hidden from view.

Accessing Popular Google+ Features

The upper-right corner of every Google+ page gives you quick access to popular Google+ features. When you click your full name or your gravatar (small photo), a pop-up box opens, as shown in Figure 1.10.

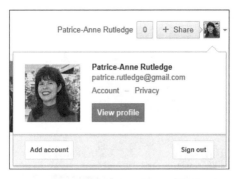

FIGURE 1.10   Quickly access popular features.

In this box, you can click the following buttons and links:

> ▶ **Notifications.** Open the Notifications menu, which displays your latest notifications. The Notifications button tells you how many

unread notifications you have by highlighting this number in red. If you don't have any unread notifications, the button displays the number zero (0) and isn't highlighted in red. See Lesson 9, "Viewing and Managing Notifications," for more information.

▶ **Share.** Open the share box where you can share text, photos, videos, and links. See Lesson 6, "Sharing Content on Google+," for more information.

▶ **Account.** Open the Account Overview page, described in Lesson 5, "Managing Google+ Settings and Privacy."

▶ **Privacy.** Open the Profile and Privacy page, described in Lesson 5.

▶ **View Profile.** Open your Google+ profile, described in Lesson 2, "Working with Google+ Profiles."

▶ **Add Account.** Open a new window that enables you to sign in to another Google account. To learn more about multiple sign-in, click the **Learn More** link.

▶ **Sign Out.** Sign out of Google+. If you're using a public computer or if other people have ready access to your own computer, you should sign out of Google+ when you're finished using it.

If you create any Google+ pages (see Lesson 3, "Creating a Google+ Page for Your Business," for more information), you will be able to access them from this pop-up box as well.

Getting Help

Although *Sams Teach Yourself Google+ in 10 Minutes, Second Edition* should provide answers to most of your Google+ questions, at times you might want to refer to online help. For example, Google+ Help keeps you updated on new Google+ features that are released after this book's publication.

To access Google+ Help, click the **Home** icon on the Google+ ribbon and select **Help** from the drop-down menu in the upper-right corner of the page (see Figure 1.11). The Google+ Help page opens, shown in Figure 1.12.

FIGURE 1.11   Access Help from this menu of options.

FIGURE 1.12   Learn what's new on Google+.

Here you can search for answers to your questions, review information about popular topics, and learn what's new on Google+.

Sending Feedback

If you run into a problem on Google+ or want to give Google suggestions about future features or improvements, you can submit feedback.

To submit feedback to Google, click the **Home** icon on the Google+ ribbon and select **Send Feedback** from the drop-down menu in the upper-right corner of the page (refer to Figure 1.11). The Google Feedback dialog box opens, shown in Figure 1.13, where you can enter your feedback. Depending on your operating system and browser, the appearance of this dialog box could vary.

FIGURE 1.13   Send Google your feedback about Google+.

> TIP: **Submit One Feedback Report per Problem**
> If you have multiple problems, submit a feedback report for each problem. This makes it easier for Google to categorize and respond to your feedback.

Summary

In this first lesson, you learned about the many features Google+ offers and how to sign up for an account. Next, it's time to create a more detailed profile.

LESSON 2
Working with Google+ Profiles

In this lesson, you learn how to edit and manage your Google+ profile.

Understanding Google+ Profiles

When you first sign up for Google+, your profile contains only basic information. Figure 2.1 shows a sample profile for a new Google+ user.

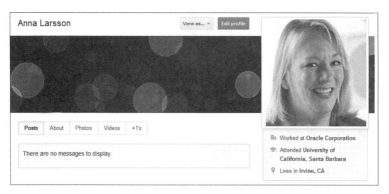

FIGURE 2.1 Your profile is a blank canvas when you first sign up for Google+.

Figure 2.2 shows a sample completed Google+ profile.

Message button

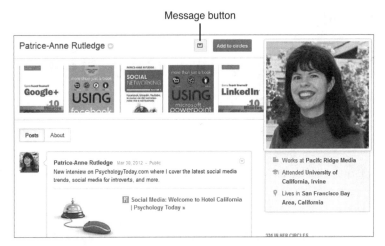

FIGURE 2.2   A complete profile lets people know who you are and generates better results.

NOTE: **Why Does My Profile Already Contain Content?**

If you created a profile using Google Profiles (https://profiles.google.com) before the launch of Google+, Google uses this content as the basis for your initial Google+ profile.

Although you can customize your profile content, all Google+ profiles follow the same basic layout:

▶ The left column displays the person's name, an optional cover photo (or scrapbook of up to five individual photos), and profile tabs with custom content. If you've added this person to a circle, the name of the circle displays; otherwise the Add to Circles button displays. Optionally, the Message button (small envelope) displays if the profile owner accepts messages on Google+.

▶ The right column displays a profile photo and basic information, photos of people from their circles, and links to send an email, block this person, or report this profile to Google+.

Before sharing content on Google+ and adding people to circles, you should enhance your profile with more detailed content and specify your preferred profile privacy settings.

As you add more content to your profile, consider carefully how you plan to use Google+. Do you want to communicate primarily with family and friends? Are you sharing content with professional colleagues? Or are you using your personal profile to promote your business? Thinking about your goals and target audience can help you determine what to post on your profile and which privacy settings to select.

> CAUTION: **Don't Use a Personal Profile to Create a Business Presence**
>
> Google+ profiles are designed for individuals using their own name. If you want to create a Google+ presence for a business, brand, or organization, you should create a Google+ page. See Lesson 3, "Creating a Google+ Page for Your Business," for more information.

Google+ enables you to edit your profile; you can choose the exact content to display on it and specify who can view it.

Adding a Profile Cover Photo

Google+ enables you to add an optional cover photo at the top of your profile. There are two options for your cover photo:

▶ A single photo, 940px by 180px in size.

▶ A scrapbook with five individual photos, sized at 110px by 110px each (refer to Figure 2.2).

If you don't add your own cover photo or scrapbook, Google+ adds a default single photo to your profile (refer to Figure 2.1 for an example).

Adding a Single Cover Photo

To add a single cover photo to your profile, follow these steps:

1. Click the **Profile** icon on the Google+ ribbon.

2. Click the **Edit Profile** button at the top of the page.

3. Click the **Change Your Cover Photo** link at the top of your
   profile.

4. Select the single photo template (on the left), as shown in
   Figure 2.3.

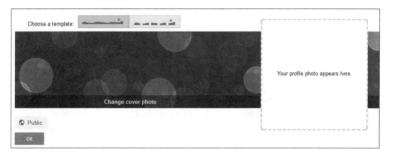

FIGURE 2.3   Choose the template to upload a single cover photo.

5. Click the **Change Your Cover Photo** link to open the Select
   Cover Photo dialog box.

6. Click the **Select a Photo from Your Computer** button to select
   photos to upload.

7. In the File Upload dialog box, select a file to upload, and click
   the **Open** button. Depending on your operating system and
   browser, the name of this dialog box and button could vary.

8. In the Select Cover Photo dialog box, shown in Figure 2.4, drag
   the four white squares that surround your photo to crop it to the
   desired size.

9. Click the **Save** button.

10. Click the **Done Editing** button at the top of your profile.

Your cover photo now displays on your photo and is available in the
Scrapbook Photos album on the Albums tab of the Photos page.

FIGURE 2.4   Display a cover photo that tells your story.

Adding a Photo Scrapbook to Your Profile

To add a photo scrapbook to your profile, follow these steps:

1. Click the **Profile** icon on the Google+ ribbon.

2. Click the **Edit Profile** button in the upper-right corner of the page.

3. Click the **Change Cover Photo** link at the top of your profile.

4. Select the scrapbook photo template (on the right).

5. Click the **Add Photo** link (see Figure 2.5) to open the Add Photos to Scrapbook dialog box.

CAUTION: **Consider Carefully Which Photos Are Appropriate for Your Scrapbook**

Displaying a public photo scrapbook at the top of your profile is optional. If you do decide to use this feature, consider carefully the photos you want to represent you and display to the public. For example, I use my profile photo scrapbook to display cover photos of my recent books.

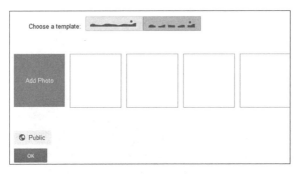

FIGURE 2.5 Add photos you already uploaded to your scrapbook or upload new photos.

6. Click the **Select a Photo from Your Computer** button to select photos to upload. You can upload photos in the following formats: JPG, GIF, or PNG.

> TIP: **Add Existing Google+ Photos to Your Scrapbook**
> To add any of your existing photos on Google+ to your scrapbook, click the **Your Photos** tab on the Add Photos to Scrapbook dialog box, select a photo, and click the **Add Photos to Scrapbook** button.

7. In the File Upload dialog box, select a file to upload, and click the **Open** button. Depending on your operating system and browser, the name of this dialog box and button could vary.

8. Continue uploading any additional photos. Google+ can display up to five photos on your profile.

9. Click the **OK** button to close the scrapbook area.

10. Click the **Done Editing** button at the top of your profile.

Your scrapbook photos now display on your photo and are available in the Scrapbook Photos album on the Albums tab of the Photos page. To rearrange the display order of your photos, click the **Manage Photos** link. See Lesson 10, "Working with Photos," for more information.

Deleting a Photo

To delete a cover or scrapbook photo, follow these steps:

1. Click the **Profile** icon on the Google+ ribbon.

2. Click the **Edit Profile** button in the upper-right corner of the page.

3. Click the **Change Photos** link.

4. To delete a cover photo, click the **Delete Photo** link and click the **Delete** button in the confirmation dialog box. From here, you can add a new cover photo, add a photo scrapbook, or use the Google+ default cover.

5. To delete an individual scrapbook photo, select the photo you want to delete, click the **Delete Photo** link that displays (see Figure 2.6), and click the **Delete** button in the confirmation dialog box. After deleting a photo, you can add a new photo to replace it.

Delete Photo link

FIGURE 2.6   Delete scrapbook photos if you want to add new ones.

6. Click the **OK** button to close the photo area.

7. Click the **Done Editing** button at the top of your profile.

Changing Your Profile Photo

When you signed up for Google+, you were prompted to add a profile photo. This photo, sized at 250px by 250px, displays on the right side of your profile (refer to Figures 2.1 and 2.2).

To change your profile photo, click the **Profile** icon on the Google+ ribbon, click the **Edit Profile** button, and click the **Change Profile Photo** link. The Select Profile Photo dialog box opens, where you can choose a new photo. See Lesson 1, "Introducing Google+," if you need a reminder about how to use the options in the Select Profile Photo dialog box.

Editing Your Name

Google+ enables you to edit your name if you don't want to display the first and last name you used when you signed up. To edit your profile name, follow these steps:

1. Click the **Profile** icon on the Google+ ribbon.

2. Click the **Edit Profile** button in the upper-right corner of the page.

3. Click your name to open a pop-up box where you can edit your first and last name. Optionally, you can click the **More Options** link to add a nickname and specify exactly how you want Google+ to display it.

CAUTION: **Read Google+ Naming Rules Before Using a Nickname**

Be sure to review Google+'s detailed naming guidelines before changing the name on your Google+ personal profile: http://support.google.com/plus/bin/answer.py?hl=en&answer=1228271. Google+ has very specific rules regarding the use of nicknames on your profile.

---

4. Click the **Save** button to save your changes and close the
   pop-up box.

5. Click the **Done Editing** button at the top of the Google+ page.

Editing Your Profile's About Tab

To edit your profile's About tab, follow these steps:

1. Click the **Profile** icon on the Google+ ribbon.

2. Click the **Edit Profile** button in the upper-right corner of the page.

3. On the **About** tab, which opens by default, click the section you
   want to edit and enter your content. Only sections for which you
   add content display on your profile. Figure 2.7 shows the sections available for edit on the About tab. The content you entered
   when you signed up for Google+ already displays here.
   Optionally, you can complete any additional fields you also want
   to display on your profile.

FIGURE 2.7   Choose the sections you want to display on your About tab.

These sections include the following:

- ▶ **Tagline.** Enter a tagline to display at the top of your About tab. Consider carefully what you want to display here. It's often the first impression people have about who you are. Think of this text as a headline. By default, your tagline is always public.

- ▶ **Introduction.** Add a paragraph or two about yourself. The Introduction dialog box includes buttons that enable you to bold, italicize, and underline text; add bulleted and numbered lists; and add links to external websites. If you make a mistake, click the **Remove Formatting** button to remove any formatting you applied. Figure 2.8 shows the Introduction dialog box.

FIGURE 2.8   You can format text and add links to your introduction.

- ▶ **Bragging Rights.** Let people know about accomplishments you're proud of—both personal and professional.

- ▶ **Occupation.** Enter your occupation or professional headline in the text box.

- ▶ **Employment.** Start typing your company name and Google+ displays potential matches from existing profiles. For example, if you work for Pearson Education, a drop-down list displays this company when you start to type its name (see Figure 2.9). Optionally, enter your title and employment dates for each job and click the **Current** check box if you're currently employed with that company. If you make a mistake, click the **Remove Item** button (**X**) to delete a row.

FIGURE 2.9   Google+ displays potential employer matches in a drop-down list.

> ▶ **Education.** Start typing your school name and Google+ displays potential matches from existing profiles. For example, if you attended Stanford University, a drop-down list displays this school when you start to type its name. Optionally, enter your major and attendance dates for each school and click the **Current** check box if you're a current student. If you make a mistake, click the **Remove Item** button (**X**) to delete a row.

> ▶ **Places Lived.** Type the names of cities where you've lived to display them on a map on your profile.

> ▶ **Home.** Enter your home contact information, such as your home phone number, mobile phone number, email address, and so forth. If you choose to enter data in this section, be sure to consider your privacy options carefully.

> ▶ **Work.** Enter your work contact information, such as your work phone number, mobile phone number, email address, and so forth. If you choose to enter data in this section, be sure to consider your privacy options carefully.

- ▶ **Relationship.** Select one of ten relationship status options if you want to broadcast your personal status to your Google+ friends.

- ▶ **Looking For.** Select one of the following relationship goals if you want to let others know what you're looking for: friends, dating, a relationship, or networking.

- ▶ **Gender.** Select one of the three options Google+ provides: male, female, or other.

- ▶ **Other Names.** Enter other names, such as a maiden name.

- ▶ **Profile Discovery**. Specify whether you want to make your profile available in search results, such as on Google, Yahoo!, or Bing. This option is most useful if you want to use your profile to promote a business or your expertise as a job candidate.

- ▶ **Other Profiles.** Display links to your website and your profiles on other social sites. See "Adding Links on Your Google+ Profile" later in this lesson for more information about adding links.

- ▶ **Contributor To.** Display links to sites you contribute to.

- ▶ **Recommended Links.** Display links to interesting websites you would recommend to others.

4. Select your privacy options for each section from the drop-down list. See "Specifying Profile Privacy by Section" next in this lesson for more information.

5. Click the **Save** button to save your changes for each section.

6. Click the **Done Editing** button at the top of the Google+ page.

Specifying Profile Privacy by Section

To specify who can view a profile section, click the drop-down list on that section to display the privacy options available (see Figure 2.10).

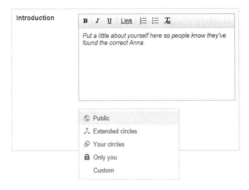

FIGURE 2.10   You have control over who sees each section of your profile.

Your options include the following:

▶ **Public.** Make the section public, available to anyone on the Web whether or not they are in your circles. This option is most suited to public figures or those who want to use their profile for marketing purposes.

▶ **Extended Circles.** Share with the people who are in your circles' circle. For example, if your friend Sara is in one of your circles, the people in her circles would also be able to view your content.

▶ **Your Circles.** Share with people in your own circles. This is the default selection.

▶ **Only You.** Ensure maximum privacy for this data. You're the only person who can view it. You can also simply delete the content in a section to remove it from your profile.

▶ **Custom.** Specify exactly who can view this section. For example, you could display a section to your "Family" and "Friends" circles, but not to your "Business" circle.

TIP: **Review Your Profile Privacy Any Time You Create New Circles**

If you want to restrict access to profile sections by circle, edit your profile again after creating new circles. See Lesson 4, "Managing Your Network with Circles," for more information about creating circles.

See Lesson 5, "Managing Google+ Settings and Privacy," for information about additional Google+ privacy options.

Adding Links on Your Google+ Profile

Adding links on your Google+ profile can help drive traffic to your other sites. You can add links to your profiles on sites such as Facebook, LinkedIn, or Twitter; sites you contribute to; or sites you recommend.

To add links on your Google+ profile, follow these steps:

1. Click one of the following About tab sections to open the related dialog box: Other Profiles, Contributor To, or Recommended Links. For example, if you click the **Other Profiles** section, the Other Profiles dialog box opens. The process for adding links to each of these sections is the same.

2. Click the **Add Custom Link** link (see Figure 2.11).

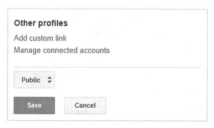

FIGURE 2.11   Link to your website, blog, or other social site.

TIP: **Let Google+ Find Potential Profile Links for You**

If you have profiles on other sites, you can let Google find them for you and add a link on your Google+ profile automatically. To do so, click the **Manage Connected Accounts** link on the Other Profiles dialog box to open the Connected Accounts page. On this page, you can connect Google+ with your profile on sites such as Facebook, Yahoo!, Flickr, LinkedIn, Quora, Twitter, Yelp, Hotmail, MySpace, Plaxo, and last.fm. For more information about connecting accounts, see Lesson 5.

3. Enter the name for your link in the first text box. For example, if you want to link to your website or blog, enter its name.

4. Enter the complete URL of your website, such as www.patricerutledge.com.

5. Repeat steps 2 through 4 until you finish adding links. You can reposition links by dragging the bar to the left of a link name (see Figure 2.12).

FIGURE 2.12   You can reposition, edit, or delete links in the Other Profiles dialog box.

6. Select your privacy options from the drop-down list. See "Specifying Profile Privacy by Section" earlier in this lesson for more information.

7. Click the **Save** button to save your changes and close the dialog box.

8. Click the **Done Editing** button at the top of the Google+ page.

Figure 2.13 shows an example of links on a Google+ profile.

FIGURE 2.13   Some sample links on a Google+ profile.

After adding links to your Google+ profile, you can:

▶ Change a link's display order by dragging the handle to the left of its name in the dialog box (refer to Figure 2.12).

▶ Edit the link content by clicking the **Edit Link** button.

▶ Delete the link by clicking the **Remove Item** button.

Specifying the Tabs to Display on Your Profile

In addition to the About tab, Google+ profiles display several other tabs. You can choose which tabs to display and who can view them.

To specify which tabs to display on your profile, follow these steps:

1. Click the **Profile** icon on the Google+ ribbon.

2. Click the **Edit Profile** button in the upper-right corner of the page.

3. Select the tab you want to edit and make any changes. These include the following:

▶ **Posts.** Google+ requires you to display the Posts tab, so there are no edit options for posts. When people click this tab, they view your Google+ posts based on the security settings you applied to them.

▶ **Photos.** The Photos tab displays photos you uploaded to Google+. If you don't want to display this tab, remove the check mark next to the Show This Tab on Your Profile check box and click the **Save** button (see Figure 2.14). The tab also enables you to:

   ▶ Allow viewers to download your photos

   ▶ Find your face in photos, prompt the people in your circles to tag you, and specify whose tags to approve automatically. See Lesson 10, for more information about photo tagging.

   ▶ Show a geographic location on the albums and photos you uploaded.

FIGURE 2.14   Control how photos display on your profile.

▶ **Videos.** The Videos tab displays videos you uploaded to Google+. If you don't want to display this tab, remove the check mark next to the Show This Tab on Your Profile check box and click the **Save** button. See Lesson 6, "Sharing Content on Google+," for more information about posting videos on Google+.

▶ **+1's.** The +1's tab displays your +1 activity across the Web. For example, if you read an interesting blog post on another website and clicked the post's +1 button to show your support, it would display on this tab. If you don't want to display the +1's tab, remove the check mark next to the Show This Tab on Your Profile check box and click the **Save** button.

4. Click the **Done Editing** button at the top of the Google+ page.

Specifying Your Contact Settings

Optionally, you can allow your profile visitors to contact you on Google+ in two ways. You can display the:

▶ Message button at the top of your profile, to the right of your name (refer to Figure 2.2). When someone sends you a message, Google+ sends you a notification. See Lesson 7, "Viewing Your Google+ Stream," for more information about notifications. No one else can view a message another user sends just to you.

▶ Send [First Name] an Email link at the bottom of the right profile column, below the photos of people in your circles. When someone sends you an email (to the email address associated with your Google+ account), Google doesn't reveal your actual email address.

Google+ enables you to control who sees these contact options on your profile: the public, people in your circles, people in your extended circles, a custom group of people, or no one.

To specify who can view these contact options on your profile, follow these steps:

1. Click the **Profile** icon on the Google+ ribbon.

2. Click the **Edit Profile** button in the upper-right corner of the page.

3. Click the **About** tab.

   4. Click the **Change Contact Settings** button.

   5. If you want to let people send you a message on Google+, select the **Allow People to Send You a Message from a Link on Your Profile** check box (see Figure 2.15).

FIGURE 2.15   You can specify who can send you a message on Google+.

   6. If you want to receive email from your Google+ profile visitors, select the **Allow People to Email You from a Link on Your Profile** check box.

   7. From the drop-down lists next to each option, specify who can view these contact options on your profile. See "Specifying Profile Privacy by Section" earlier in this lesson for more information about each option.

   8. Click the **Save** button to save your changes.

   9. Click the **Done Editing** button at the top of the page.

Specifying the People to Display on Your Profile

When someone visits your Google+ profile, the right column displays photos of the people you share in common, the people in your circles, and the people who have you in their circles. Hovering over someone's photo opens a pop-up box with more information about that person. If you want to restrict who can view your Google+ network or remove this section from your profile completely, you can do so.

To specify the people who display on your profile and who can view them, follow these steps:

1. Click the **Profile** icon on the Google+ ribbon.

2. Click the **Edit Profile** button in the upper-right corner of the page.

3. Click the **In Your Circles** text on the right column of your profile.

4. Verify that the **In Your Circles** check box is selected if you want to display people in your circles on your profile (see Figure 2.16). Otherwise, remove the check mark next to this check box and skip to step 7.

FIGURE 2.16   Determine which people display on your profile.

5. From the drop-down box, select which circles you want to display. You can display people in all circles or only selected circles. For example, you might want to display business associates but not family members.

6. Specify who can see this section on your profile: anyone on the Web (public) or only people in your circles.

7. Click the **Save** button to save your changes.

8. Click the **Have You in Circles** text on the right column of your profile.

9. Verify that the **Have You in Circles** check box is selected if you want to display the people who have you in circles on your profile. Otherwise, remove the check mark next to this check box.

10. Click the **Save** button to save your changes.

11. Click the **Done Editing** button at the top of the page.

Viewing Your Profile as Others See It

After you finish making edits to your page, you might want to see how your profile changes display to others.

To view your Google+ profile as others see it, follow these steps:

1. Click the **Profile** icon on the Google+ ribbon.

2. Click the **View As** button at the top of the page.

3. Click the **Public** button to view the public version of your profile (see Figure 2.17).

FIGURE 2.17   You can preview how your profile looks to the world—or to a specific person.

4. If you want to preview how your profile displays to a specific person (such as someone in one of your circles), start typing that person's name in the text box. Google+ searches for and displays matches in your circle. Click the name of a person to view your profile as that person sees it.

5. If your profile displays unexpected results, click the **Edit Profile** button to make profile changes.

6. When you're finished previewing your profile, select **Stop Viewing as Public** from the Viewing as Public drop-down menu.

Adding a Google+ Profile Button to Your Website

If you want to attract more people to your Google+ profile, you can add a Google+ profile button to your website or blog. Adding this button is also a good way to identify site ownership so that your website content displays on the +1's tab of your Google+ profile. To do so, visit the Google Profile Button page at www.google.com/webmasters/profilebutton. If you use WordPress, consider adding a googleCard to your sidebar using the googleCards plugin (http://plusdevs.com/google-wordpress-plugin).

Summary

In this lesson, you learned how to edit and manage your profile. Next, learn how to create a Google+ page for a business, a brand, or an organization.

LESSON 3

Creating a Google+ Page for Your Business

In this lesson, you learn how to create a Google+ page for your business, brand, or organization.

Understanding Google+ Pages Versus Google+ Profiles

At first, the difference between a Google+ page and a Google+ profile seems pretty clear. A *profile* is for an individual person and a *page* is for a business, brand, or organization. In addition, Google+ identifies pages with the Google+ Pages icon, which displays to the right of the page name, as shown in Figure 3.1.

FIGURE 3.1 Google identifies pages with a square icon.

When you pause your mouse over the square gray icon, it changes color and displays the word "page" next to it.

There are other more important differences between pages and profiles, however. Table 3.1 offers a quick overview of these differences.

TABLE 3.1   Differences Between Google+ Profiles and Google+ Pages

Feature	Google+ Profile	Google+ Page
Add pages to your circles	Yes	Yes
Add profiles to your circles	Yes	Yes, but only if profile owners mention your page or add it to one of their circles first
Participate in games	Yes	No
Share to extended circles	Yes	No
Participate in a hangout from a mobile device	Yes	No
Click the +1 button to support pages and posts	Yes	No
Display the +1 button below your logo for visitors to click	No	Yes

Understanding what you can—and can't—do with a Google+ page is critical to your page's success. This knowledge makes it easier to develop a solid Google+ page strategy and to integrate your page with your profile—and the profiles of those who work for your company.

Creating a Google+ Page

To create a Google+ page, follow these steps:

1. Sign into Google+ using the account of the person you want to be the owner of this page.

> TIP: **Choose Your Page Owner Wisely**
>
> If you're creating a Google+ page for your own business, you'll most likely use your own Google account. If you're creating a page for a larger organization, consider carefully who the page owner should be. Although you can add other page managers later or transfer page ownership to another person, it's important to choose your

initial page owner wisely and give this responsibility to someone
with the professionalism and insight required to represent your
organization to the world.

2. Click the **Pages** icon on the Google+ ribbon. If this icon doesn't
   display on the ribbon, click the **More** icon and select **Pages** from
   the pop-out menu.

3. On the right side of the page, click the **Create New Page** button.
   Optionally, navigate to https://plus.google.com/u/0/pages/create.

4. On the Create a Google+ Page page, select a category for your
   Google+ page. Your options include: Local Business or Place;
   Product or Brand; Company, Institution, or Organization; Arts,
   Entertainment, or Sports; or Other.

5. Google+ displays additional fields on the right side of the page,
   which vary based on your category selection. For most category
   types, Google+ asks for a page name, website URL, subcategory,
   and the age range of your intended audience. If you want to create a page for a local business or place, you're prompted to enter
   your phone number. Figure 3.2 shows an example of the fields
   that display for the Company, Institution, or Organization category. Enter the fields required for your category type.

6. Click the **Pages Terms** link to review Google's Terms of Service
   for pages and then click the check box to verify that you understand these terms.

7. Click the **Create** button to create your page. Figure 3.3 displays
   a new Google+ page.

8. Enter a tagline for your business of up to 10 words. You can use
   the tagline from your website or create a phrase using keywords
   relevant to your page.

9. Click the **Set Profile Photo** button to open the Select Profile
   Photo dialog box where you can upload a logo or other image to
   represent your page (see Figure 3.4). Google+ sizes this image at
   250 by 250 pixels.

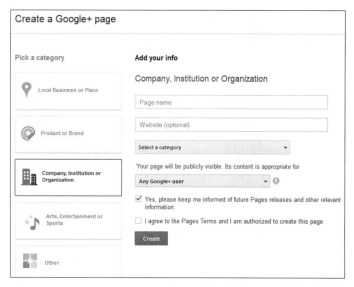

FIGURE 3.2   Complete the fields required for the category type you choose.

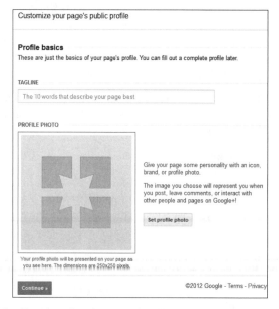

FIGURE 3.3   Your new Google+ page is a blank canvas.

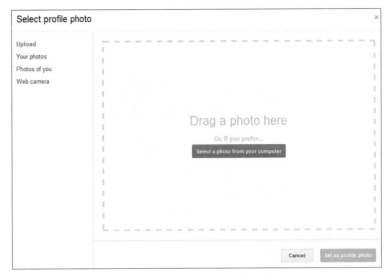

FIGURE 3.4   Select a photo to display on your Google+ page.

10. Click the **Select a Photo from Your Computer** button.

11. In the File Upload dialog box, select the photo you want to upload and click the **Open** button. Depending on your browser and operating system, this dialog box and button could have different names.

12. In the Select Profile Photo dialog box, shown in Figure 3.5, drag the four white squares that surround your photo to crop it to the desired size.

> TIP: **Quickly Fix Problems with Your Photo**
>
> Optionally, you can click the **Left** or **Right** buttons next to your photo to fix rotation problems. If you need to fix cosmetic issues, such as red eye or color contrast, click the **Creative Kit** button.

13. Click the **Set as Profile Photo** button. Google+ returns to the Customize Your Page's Public Profile page where your photo now displays.

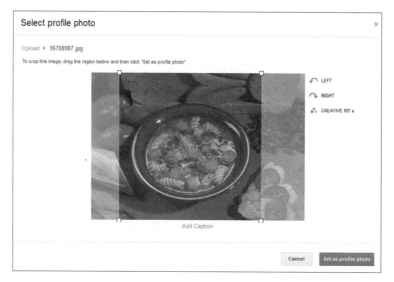

FIGURE 3.5   Crop your photo to fit in the space provided.

14. Click the **Continue** button to continue to the Get the Word Out page, which prompts you to tell your circles about this page. Instead, I recommend that you wait to notify the world about your page until it contains additional content.

15. Click the **Finish** button to complete your page. Google+ opens the Get Started page, as shown in Figure 3.6.

From this page, you can do the following:

▶ **Add page profile content.** Click the **Profile** icon on the Google+ ribbon to open the Profile page. Here you can add content to your page's About tab and create a photo scrapbook that brands your business. Adding content to your page's profile content is very similar to adding content to your personal profile. See Lesson 2, "Working with Google+ Profiles," for more information.

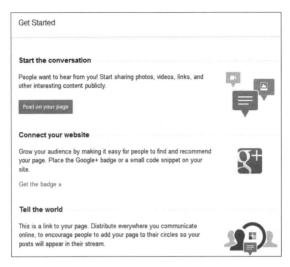

FIGURE 3.6   Google+ offers many choices after you create a basic page.

> TIP: **Maximize the Potential of Your Page's Cover Photo or Scrapbook**
>
> To make the most of the opportunity that a cover photo or scrap-book provides, get creative and select photos that best match the business image and message you want to convey. Depending on the type of business you have, you could display photos of your products, text-based images that describe your services, photos of key personnel, and so forth. See Lesson 2 for more information about adding a cover photo or scrapbook (the process is nearly identical for both pages and profiles).

▶ **Create circles and add pages and people to them.** Click the **Circles** icon on the Google+ ribbon to open the Circles page. Although Google+ offers different default circles for pages (Following, Customers, VIPs, and Team Members), they work in much the same way as circles for profiles. Remember, however, that you can add profiles to one of your circles only if the profile owners mention your page or add it to one of their circles first. There are no limits for adding other pages to your circles. See

Lesson 4, "Managing Your Network with Circles," for more information about Google+ circles.

▶ **Start posting content on your page.** Click the **Post on Your Page** button to go to your stream where you can post your own content. Optionally, click the **Promote Your Page** link to the right of your page's share box to create a post on your personal profile, letting others know about your new page. See Lesson 6, "Sharing Content on Google+," for more information about posting content on Google+.

▶ **Connect your Google+ page to your website.** Click the **Get the Badge** link to open the Link Your Google+ Page to Your Site page, which provides the code for several badge styles, including one that displays a +1 button encouraging site visitors to recommend your site.

Using Google+ as a Page

When you manage your own profile as well as one or more pages on Google+, it's important to distinguish whether you're posting content as yourself or as a page you manage. The easiest way to post as a page is to sign in to Google+ and navigate directly to your page. If you're currently using your Google+ profile, pause your mouse over the **Pages** icon on the Google+ ribbon and select the page you want to use from the Pages pop-out menu that displays (see Figure 3.7).

FIGURE 3.7   Selecting a Google+ page from your profile.

You can also click your name or photo in the upper-right corner of the page to select your page.

TIP: **Gain Quick Access to Multiple Pages**
If you manage multiple Google+ pages, click the **Pages** icon on the Google+ ribbon to open the Manage Your Pages page, which gives you easy access to all your pages. You can also access this page by clicking the All Your Google+ Pages link on the pop-up box that displays when you click your name or photo in the upper-right corner of any Google+ page.

After opening your Google+ page, a notification at the top of the screen informs you that you're using Google+ as a page, and anything you post will list that page as the post author.

Managing Your Google+ Page Settings

To manage your Google+ page settings, select **Settings** from the drop-down menu in the upper-right corner of your page. The Google+ Settings tab displays by default, as shown in Figure 3.8.

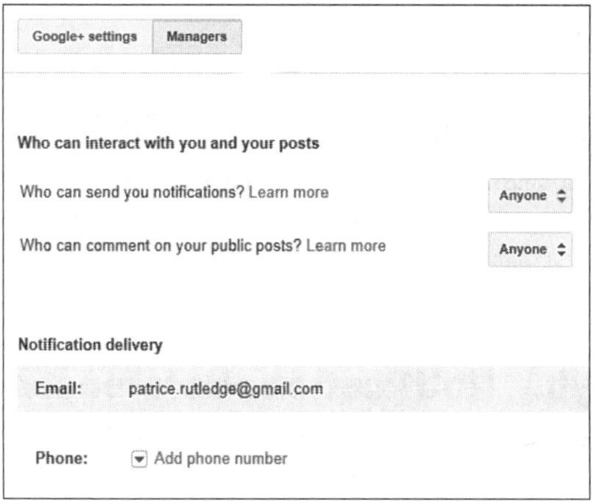

| Google+ settings | Managers |

Who can interact with you and your posts

Who can send you notifications? Learn more   Anyone ⇕

Who can comment on your public posts? Learn more   Anyone ⇕

Notification delivery

Email: patrice.rutledge@gmail.com

Phone: ⊡ Add phone number

FIGURE 3.8   Specify the settings for your Google+ page.

On this page, you can specify who can interact with your posts, add email addresses for notification delivery, customize what Google+ includes in the Your Circles option, and specify photo settings.

Specifying Who Can Interact with You and Your Posts

The Who Can Interact with You and Your Posts section enables you to control exactly who can send you notifications and comment on your public posts. Your choices include: Anyone, Your Circles, Only You, or Custom (this gives you the option of selecting specific circles or people). By default, Google+ allows anyone to send you notifications and to comment on your public posts.

Specifying Your Notification Delivery Preferences

The Notification Delivery section lists the email address associated with the person who created your page. To add another email address, click the **Change** link, enter a new email address in the text box, and click the **Add** button.

If you prefer receiving notifications via text message, click the **Add Phone Number** link to enter your mobile phone number.

Managing Your Email Subscriptions

By default, Google+ sends you occasional updates about top content from your circles, Google+ activity, and friend suggestions. If you don't want to receive these updates, remove the check marks in the Manage Email Subscriptions section.

Specifying Notification Preferences

The Receive Notifications section enables you to specify which actions trigger a Google+ notification and how to send this notification: by email, via SMS text message, or both. This section displays the events that trigger notifications, such as when someone mentions your page in a post, adds your page to a circle, tags your page, comments on one of your posts, and so forth.

For each event, you can select your preferred notification method. If you don't want to receive any notifications, remove the check marks from all check boxes.

> NOTE: **Why Can't I Select the Phone Check Box?**
> You must select the SMS option button in the Notification Delivery section at the top of this tab to activate the Phone column.

Customizing Your Circles

By default, when you choose to share content with Your Circles, Google+ shares with all your circles except the Following circle. To customize this, click the **Customize** button in the Your Circles section. In the pop-up box that opens, you can select the specific circles you want to include in Your Circles.

Managing Photo Settings

Optionally, Google+ enables you to:

▶ Show your photos' geographic location in newly uploaded albums and photos.

▶ Allow viewers to download your photos.

▶ Find your face in photos, prompt people in your circles to tag you, and specify whose tags to approve automatically.

To enable any of these options, place a check mark in the associated check box.

Deleting a Google+ Page

If you no longer want to keep your Google+ page, you can delete it. Note that deleting a page does not delete the Google+ profile of the person who created it. Only page owners can delete a page; page managers cannot.

To delete your Google+ page, click the **Delete Page** link at the bottom of the page and click the **Yes** button to confirm page deletion.

Google+ suggests transferring ownership of a page as an alternative to deletion. To learn more about transferring ownership of your Google+, see "Transferring Ownership of a Google+ Page" later in this lesson.

Adding Google+ Page Managers

If you want to share the responsibility of managing your Google+ page with others in your organization, you can add one or more page managers. Although having a backup plan for your Google+ page is a good idea, I recommend limiting access to your page to just a few selected individuals who have the knowledge and professionalism to represent your organization publicly. To add another manager to your page, follow these steps:

1. Select **Settings** from the drop-down menu in the upper-right corner of your page.

2. Select the **Managers** tab.

TIP: **Page Managers Don't Have the Same Access Rights as Page Owners**

Although the people you designate as managers have the right to post content, edit circles, and take other actions on behalf of a page, only the page owner (the person who created the page) can transfer ownership or delete the page. For more information about the roles and capabilities of page managers, click the **Learn More** link on the Managers tab.

---

3. Enter the email address of the person you want to add as a page manager, as shown in Figure 3.9.

4. Click the **Invite** button.

5. In the pop-up box that opens, click the **Invite** button to confirm your invitation.

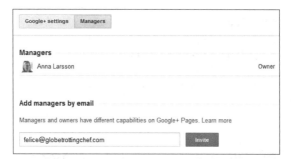

FIGURE 3.9   Invite other people to become a Google+ page manager.

Google+ sends an email that prompts this person to click the Become a Manager button in the invite and accept the terms and conditions for Google+ pages. Note that a page manager must already have a Google+ account or sign up for one to become a page manager.

The person you invited displays on the Managers tab with the status of Invited until accepting this email invite. After that, the Invited status disappears and the page manager can begin managing the page.

Removing a Google+ Manager

If a Google+ page manager leaves your company or no longer needs access to your page, you can remove this person as a manager.

To remove a Google+ manager, follow these steps:

1. Select **Settings** from the drop-down menu in the upper-right corner of your page.

2. Select the **Managers** tab.

3. Click the **Remove** button (x) to the right of the manager you want to delete.

4. In the pop-up box, click the **Remove** button to permanently remove this person as a page manager.

NOTE: **What Happens to a Deleted Manager's Posts?**
When you delete a Google+ page manager, this person can no longer post content or comments on behalf of that page. All of a previous manager's content remains on the page, however. If you want to delete this person's posts and comments, you must do so manually.

Transferring Ownership of a Google+ Page

The role of a page owner is an important one. The page owner is the only person who can transfer ownership or delete a page. If you need to change ownership of a page to another person, however, you can do so. For example, if a page owner leaves your company, you might want to transfer ownership to one of your other page managers.

To transfer ownership of a Google+ page, follow these steps:

1. Select **Settings** from the drop-down menu in the upper-right corner of your page.

2. Select the **Managers** tab.

3. Click the **Transfer Ownership** link in the upper-right corner of the page. This link doesn't display unless you have at least one page manager (in addition to the page owner).

4. In the pop-up box, select the manager to whom you want to transfer ownership and click the **Continue** button (see Figure 3.10).

5. Click the **OK** button to confirm the transfer.

After transferring page ownership, the prior owner becomes a manager. You also can remove this person as a manager if he or she is no longer involved with your company. See "Removing a Google+ Manager" earlier in this lesson for more information.

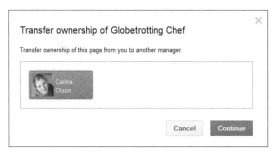

FIGURE 3.10   Transfer ownership of a Google+ page to another page manager.

Summary

In this lesson, you learned how to participate, create, and manage a Google+ page. Next, it's time to start using Google+ circles.

LESSON 4

Managing Your Network with Circles

In this lesson, you learn how to add and manage Google+ circles.

Understanding Google+ Circles

One of the first things to do when you sign up for Google+ is to add people you know—and those whose posts you find interesting—to circles.

> PLAIN ENGLISH: **Google+ Circles**
> **Circles** enable you to organize your Google+ network by placing people into distinct groups. When you post content on Google+, you can specify exactly which circles can view those posts. You can also specify privacy settings by circle. This gives you complete control over who sees what content.

By default, Google+ offers four ready-made circles for your profile (the default circles for pages are different), but you can also create new circles and delete any circles you don't want to use. The default circles are shown in Figure 4.1:

▶ **Friends.** People you consider close friends. This circle should be the one you want to give the most access to your Google+ content.

▶ **Family.** Family members, including siblings, parents, cousins, and so forth. If what you share with family members varies, consider placing them in separate circles. For example, the content you share with your sister could differ from what you share with your grandmother.

FIGURE 4.1   Google+ gets you started with four ready-made circles.

▶ **Acquaintances.** People you know who aren't close friends or family members. This circle could include coworkers, classmates, or people you know from professional associations, clubs, or community organizations. Creating separate circles for acquaintances based on shared interests is another option. For example, you might create one circle for professional colleagues and another for acquaintances you met through your love for skiing.

▶ **Following.** People whose posts you want to read on Google+, but don't actually know. Celebrities, industry experts, and popular bloggers all fall into this category.

To get started with Google+ circles, you should follow these steps:

1. Think about how you want to use Google+ and what circles you'll need.

2. Create any new circles.

3. Add people to your circles.

Creating New Circles

When you first start using Google+, you can add people to any of the default circles: Friends, Family, Acquaintances, or Following. Although these four circles might be sufficient for your needs, you can create other circles if you want to categorize people further, such as create a circle for the members of your book club or one for the members of a committee you are on.

To create a new circle, follow these steps:

1. Click the **Circles** icon on the Google+ ribbon.

2. Click the circle named **Drop Here to Create a Circle** (refer to Figure 4.1).

3. In the pop-up box that opens (see Figure 4.2), enter a name and optional description for your circle.

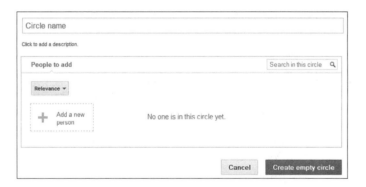

FIGURE 4.2   Give your circle an appropriate name.

4. Optionally, you can click the **Add a New Person** link to search for people by name or email address. If you want to use another method to add people to circles, click the **Create Empty Circle** button. Your new circle now displays on the Circles page.

TIP: **Create a New Circle and Add Someone to It at the Same Time**

If you already know someone you want to add to a circle (such as a person who displays on the Find People tab), you can save time by doing two things at once. Drag the person you want to add to the circle named Drop Here to Create a Circle (refer to Figure 4.1). Google+ enables you to create a circle and adds this person to it.

Adding People to Circles

When you first sign up for Google+, your circles are empty (refer to Figure 4.1). It's easy to add people to circles, but first you have to find them. Google+ offers several ways to find people to add to circles:

▶ Add people who display on the Find People tab on the Circles page.

▶ Add your email contacts.

▶ Add people and pages suggested on the right side of your Google+ home page.

▶ Add people who appear on your Notifications menu, which you can open by clicking the Notifications button located in the upper-right corner of Google+.

▶ Add people from the Explore page and What's Hot stream. See Lesson 7, "Viewing Your Google+ Stream," for more information about this stream.

▶ Add people from their Google+ profile. Many people now display a Google+ button on their website or blog, which makes it easy for you to find their profile.

▶ Send invitations to people who don't use Google+ yet and add them to your circles.

When you add people to circles, Google+ notifies them (on their Notification menu and via email) but doesn't tell them the name of the circle you added them to. For example, if you create an Annoying People circle, no one knows you placed them there.

In addition, adding people to a circle doesn't mean that you are automatically added to their circles. They must take the action to add you to their circles. In this way, adding people to Google+ circles is similar to following people on Twitter. Just because you follow them doesn't mean that they follow you.

Adding People to Circles from the Find People Tab

Discovering people to add to your circles on the Find People tab is one of the easiest ways to get started growing your Google+ circles.

To add people from the Find People tab, follow these steps:

1. Click the **Circles** icon on the Google+ ribbon.

2. Review the people on the Find People tab to locate individuals you want to add to circles. Figure 4.3 shows an example with several people waiting for you to add them to your circles. If the Email icon displays in the lower-right corner, this means that the person isn't on Google+. You can share with these people via email or invite them to join Google+.

Email link

FIGURE 4.3   The Find People tab suggests people you might want to add to your circles.

search for and add people to your circles. After you have some people in circles, the Find People tab will start displaying additional
people for you to consider.

3. If the Find People tab page contains a large number of people, you
    can narrow your results by email account or search for coworkers
    or classmates from the All Suggestions drop-down menu.

4. If you want to see more people on the Find People tab, you can
    type the name of a person in the text box or drag one of the peo-
    ple on this tab to the "Drag People Here for Related Suggestions"
    text. This displays suggestions related to that person (usually
    people in their circles).

5. Select and drag people to the appropriate circles using your
    mouse. If you want to add more than one person to a particular
    circle, select multiple people and drag the group to the desired
    circle. You can also add an individual to more than one circle.

Figure 4.4 shows a person added to a circle. On the Find People tab, a
small circle displays in the lower-right corner of the box surrounding anyone you've added to a circle.

FIGURE 4.4   The people you add to a circle display in that circle's ring.

Understanding Google+ Suggestions

The people Google+ displays on the Find People tab come from many
sources. These include the following:

▶ **People who are in your email address book.** Initially, Google+
   searches for your contacts using the email address associated

with your Google+ account. For example, if you signed up for Google+ with your Gmail address, your Gmail contacts display on the Find People tab. You can also search for your Hotmail or Yahoo! Mail contacts or upload an email address book. See "Adding Your Email Contacts" later in this lesson.

▶ People you've interacted with on Google+ or other Google products, including any connected accounts.

▶ People in your extended circles.

PLAIN ENGLISH: **Extended Circles**

Extended Circles include the people who are in your circles' circles. For example, after you add people to circles, the people in their circles are in your extended circle. Think of them as friends of friends, or friends of the people you follow on Google+.

Deleting People on the Find People Tab

Adding the people Google+ suggests on the Find People tab is optional. You can ignore any suggestion or delete the box for that person by pausing over it with your mouse and clicking the **Delete** button (x) in the upper-right corner, as shown in Figure 4.5.

FIGURE 4.5   You can delete suggested people you don't know or don't want to add to a circle.

Adding Your Email Contacts

If the Find People tab doesn't display enough people, you can search additional email accounts for more people to add to circles. Google+ enables you to search Yahoo! Mail or Hotmail for contacts or upload your email address book from Outlook, Thunderbird, Apple Address Book, and other email systems.

NOTE: **Connecting with Your Email Contacts on Google+**
After importing your email contacts, you can add them to your Google+ circles. If they have a Google+ account, they can view your posts on their stream. Otherwise, you can optionally share with them via email or send them an invitation to Google+. To invite an email contact to Google+, double-click this person's name and click the **Invite** button in the Invite People to Join You on Google+ dialog box, which opens.

Adding Your Hotmail Contacts

If you use Hotmail, you can search for and display your email contacts on the Find People tab.

To add your Hotmail contacts to circles, follow these steps:

1. Click the **Circles** icon on the Google+ ribbon.

2. On the Find People tab, select **Hotmail** from the All Suggestions drop-down menu.

3. In the pop-up box that opens, enter your Windows Live ID and password and click the **Sign In** button. Google+ connects with Hotmail and displays your email contacts on the Find People tab.

4. Google+ identifies a Hotmail contact by placing the orange Hotmail icon in the upper-right corner of the box that surrounds that person. Select and drag people to the appropriate circles using your mouse.

Adding Your Yahoo! Mail Contacts

If you use Yahoo! Mail, you can search for and display your email contacts on the Find People tab.

To add your Yahoo! Mail contacts to circles, follow these steps:

1. Click the **Circles** icon on the Google+ ribbon.

2. On the Find people tab, select **Yahoo!** from the All Suggestions drop-down menu.

3. In the pop-up box that opens, enter your Yahoo! ID and password and click the **Sign In** button.

4. Click the **Agree** button to give Yahoo! permission to share your data. Google+ connects with Yahoo! and displays your email contacts on the Find People tab.

5. Google+ identifies a Yahoo! contact by placing the purple Yahoo! icon in the upper-right corner of the box that surrounds that person. Select and drag people to the appropriate circles using your mouse.

Adding Email Contacts from an Exported File

If you use another email application—such as Outlook, Thunderbird, or Apple Mail, you can upload and display your email contacts on the Find People tab. This process works with any email system that allows you to export your data in either comma-separated values (.csv) or vCard (.vcf) format.

To add your email contacts to circles, follow these steps:

1. Export your email contacts in either .csv or .vcf format, following the instructions your email system provides.

2. Click the **Circles** icon on the Google+ ribbon.

3. On the Find People tab, select **Upload Address Book** from the All Suggestions drop-down menu and click the **Upload Address Book** link.

4. In the File Upload dialog box, select your email contact file and click the **Open** button. Depending on your operating system and browser, the name of this dialog box and button could vary. Google+ uploads your email file and displays your email contacts on the Find People tab (see Figure 4.6).

FIGURE 4.6 Add your email contacts to circles.

5. Google+ identifies any uploaded email contact by placing the green file icon in the upper-right corner of the box that surrounds that person. Select and drag people to the appropriate circles using your mouse.

Adding People and Pages that Google+ Suggests

On the right side of your home page, Google+ suggests people you may know as well as other people and pages you might enjoy based on the content you post (see Figure 4.7). To add a person, click the **Add** button and select the circle to which you want to add this individual. To check out fun and interesting people and pages, click the associated **View** button.

FIGURE 4.7   Select the circle to which you want to add this person or page.

Adding People from the Notifications Menu

You can also add people to circles from the Notifications menu. This enables you to see who has added you to their circles and decide whether you want to do the same.

To add people from the Notifications menu, follow these steps:

1. Click the **Notifications** button that displays in the upper-right corner of the screen, as shown in Figure 4.8. See Lesson 9,

"Viewing and Managing Notifications," for more information about Google+ notifications.

Notifications button

FIGURE 4.8 Click the Notifications button to display a list of your notifications.

2. Pause your mouse over the gravatar (small photo) of the person you want to add to one of your circles. A small pop-up box opens (see Figure 4.9), displaying this person's name, a larger photo, the number of other Google+ users you share in common, and the Add button.

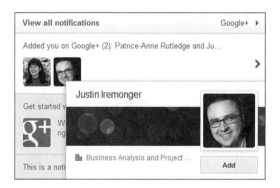

FIGURE 4.9 View people associated with recent notifications.

3. Pause your mouse over the **Add** button next to the name of a person you want to add to a circle. Google+ opens a pop-up box that lists your available circles.

4. Select the check box to the left of the circle to which you want to add this person and then move your mouse away. Google+ adds this person to the selected circle.

Optionally, you can add someone to a new circle by clicking the **Create New Circle** link in the pop-up box, typing the name of the new circle, and clicking the **Create** button.

Adding People from Their Google+ Profile

When you discover Google+ profiles of interesting people, you might want to add them to one of your circles to keep track of what they post.

To add people from their Google+ profiles, follow these steps:

1. Navigate to the Google+ profile of the person you want to add to a circle. You can find profiles by

   ▶ Searching for someone in the Search Google+ box at the top of Google+. See Lesson 8, "Searching on Google+," for more information.

   ▶ Exploring Google+ for interesting people.

   ▶ Searching for someone on Google (www.google.com).

   ▶ Clicking a Google+ button or googleCard on someone's website or blog.

2. Pause your mouse over the **Add to Circles** button in the upper-right corner of the profile whose owner you want to add to a circle, as shown in Figure 4.10. Google+ opens a pop-up box that lists your available circles.

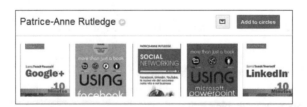

FIGURE 4.10   When you view an interesting Google+ profile, you can add this person to one of your circles.

3. Select the check box to the left of the circle to which you want to add this person and then move the mouse away. Google+ adds this person to the selected circle.

Managing Circles

Google+ makes it easy to view and manage the people in your circles. You can move people to other circles, remove individuals from circles, and delete circles.

Viewing People in Your Circles

To view the people in your circles, click the **Circles** icon on the Google+ ribbon. The Your Circles tab displays by default (see Figure 4.11).

FIGURE 4.11   View the people you added to circles.

To arrange the order in which people appear on this tab, select one of the following options from the Relevance drop-down list: First Name, Last Name, Relevance (the default), Recently Updated, Circles, and Not Yet Using Google+.

Viewing People Who Added You to Their Circles

To view the people who have added you to their circles, click the **Circles** icon on the Google+ ribbon and then click the **Have You in Circles** tab (see Figure 4.12).

FIGURE 4.12   See who has added you to their circles.

To arrange the order in which people appear on this tab, select one of the following options from the Relevance drop-down list: First Name, Last Name, Relevance, Recently Updated, and Not Yet in Circles.

Moving People from One Circle to Another

If you add someone to the wrong circle or decide you want to rearrange your circles, you can move people easily.

To move someone from one circle to another, follow these steps:

1. Click the **Circles** icon on the Google+ ribbon.

2. Click the **Your Circles** tab.

3. Drag the photo of the person you want to move from its existing circle to another circle using your mouse (see Figure 4.13).

Drag from this circle...   To this circle

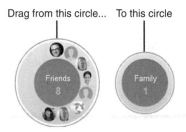

FIGURE 4.13   Drag a photo from one circle to another to move that person to another circle.

Removing People from Circles

You can remove people from a circle if you decide you no longer want to view their posts.

To remove someone from a circle, follow these steps:

1. Click the **Circles** icon on the Google+ ribbon.

2. Click the **Your Circles** tab.

3. Drag the photo of the person you want to remove away from the circle. Google+ removes the person from the circle.

CAUTION: **Where Did That Person Go?**

People you remove from a specific circle who are part of other circles remain in those other circles. If you remove people from the only circle they are part of, you remove them entirely from the Circles page. If you change your mind or remove someone by mistake, you need to search for this person again using the Search Google+ box at the top of Google+.

Editing a Circle's Name and Description

You can edit the name and description of your circles.

To edit a circle, follow these steps:

1. Click the **Circles** icon on the Google+ ribbon.

2. Right-click the circle you want to edit and select **Edit Circle** from the menu that displays, as shown in Figure 4.14.

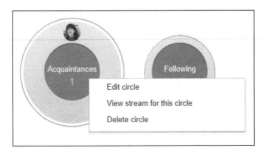

FIGURE 4.14   You can edit any circle's name or description.

3. In the pop-up box that opens, replace the existing name and description with new content.

4. Click the **Save** button to save your changes and close the dialog box.

In each circle's dialog box, at the bottom, you can click additional links to view the stream for this circle, view circle members on a tab, or delete the circle.

Deleting a Circle

If you no longer plan to use a circle, or created it by mistake, you can delete it.

To delete a circle, follow these steps:

1. Click the **Circles** icon on the Google+ ribbon.

2. Right-click the circle you want to delete and select **Delete Circle** from the menu that displays (refer to Figure 4.14).

3. In the pop-up box that opens, click the **Delete Circle** button to permanently delete the circle.

CAUTION: **Think Twice Before Deleting a Circle**

Deleting a circle with no people or that you created by mistake usually has no negative consequences. But if you delete a circle with people in it and you have shared content with this circle, you lose your connection to these people and they can no longer view anything you shared with them. Google+ circle deletions are permanent.

Sharing a Circle

If you've created a circle that you think might interest other Google+ users, you can share it. Sharing a circle is most appropriate for circles you've created on a specialized topic, such as technology journalists, small business experts, or foodies, for example. You wouldn't want to publicly share a circle that contains your family, friends, or other personal contacts.

To share a circle, follow these steps:

1. Click the **Circles** icon on the Google+ ribbon.

2. Click the circle you want to share and then click the **Share Circle** button in that circle, as shown in Figure 4.15.

FIGURE 4.15   Share interesting circles with other Google+ users.

3. In the Share Circle dialog box (see Figure 4.16), add an optional comment to let people know why you're sharing this circle.

FIGURE 4.16   Select the people with whom you want to share a circle.

4. Specify who you want to share this circle with. Your options include the following:

▶ **People in specific circles.** To share this circle with specific circles, click the **Add More People** link. In the menu that opens, select the circles you want to share with. When you're finished selecting circles, click outside the menu to close it.

▶ **A specific person.** This is the equivalent of sending a private message on Google+. If the person you want to share with uses Google+, type the person's name in the text box and select from the pop-up menu of potential matches.

5. If you want to be included in this circle, select the **Include Yourself in Shared Circle** check box.

6. Click the **Share** button. Your circle suggestion displays on the stream of the people you shared with.

Summary

In this lesson, you learned how to manage your Google+ circles. Next, you'll focus on managing your Google+ privacy settings.

LESSON 5

Managing Google+ Settings and Privacy

In this lesson, you learn how to manage your Google+ account and privacy settings.

Understanding Google+ Privacy

With Google+, you have complete control over who sees your content through a combination of Google+ circles and Google privacy settings. The Google Accounts page offers seven tabs that enable you to manage your account and privacy settings for Google+ and other connected Google products. Before you start sharing content on Google+, you should review the information and settings on this page to ensure that you understand all the available options and make the right choices for your needs.

> TIP: **What Is Google's Privacy Policy for the Content I Share on Google+?**
> For a summary of how Google uses and protects your data, read the Google+ Privacy Policy at www.google.com/policies. This page explains in plain English how Google+ uses your data.

Managing Your Google Account Settings

To manage your Google account settings, click the **Home** icon on the Google+ ribbon, select **Settings** from the drop-down menu in the upper-right corner of the page (see Figure 5.1), and click the **Account** tab on the Google Accounts page.

FIGURE 5.1   Easily access your Google+ account settings.

On the Account tab, shown in Figure 5.2, you can do the following:

▶ **Edit your profile.** Click the **Edit Profile** link to open your Google+ profile. See Lesson 2, "Working with Google+ Profiles," for more information about editing your profile.

▶ **Add an alternate email to your account.** Click the **Edit** link in the Email Addresses and Usernames section, enter an additional email address in the Add an Alternate Email to Your Account section, and click the **Save** button. An alternate email address enables you to sign in to your Google account if you can no longer access your primary email account.

▶ **Enable +1 on Non-Google Sites.** See "Enabling +1 Personalization" later in this lesson to learn how to enable or disable this feature.

FIGURE 5.2   The Account tab provides links to Google pages that help you manage your account.

▶ **Connect your accounts from other services.** Click the
Connecting Your Accounts link to open the Connected
Accounts page where you can connect Google to your accounts
on other sites such as Facebook, LinkedIn, Quora, Twitter,
Yahoo!, and more. By connecting accounts, you can view con-
tents your friends share when you search on Google. You can
also choose whether to display links to these accounts on your
Google+ profile and whether to allow Google+ to use your email
address to search for your accounts on other social sites.

▶ **Delete your Google+ profile.** See "Deleting Your Google+
Profile" later in this section for more information.

▶ **Delete your Google account.** See "Deleting Your Google
Account" later in this section for more information.

▶ **View, enable, or disable web history.** Click the **Go to Web
History** link to specify whether you want to enable this feature.

Deleting Your Google+ Profile

If you decide you no longer want to maintain your Google+ profile, you
can delete it.

> TIP: **Consider Other Options Before Deleting Your Google+
> Profile**
>
> If you're thinking about deleting your Google+ profile for privacy con-
> cerns, another option is to disable search engine visibility and
> change the visibility settings for your profile. That way, you can
> retain a profile but have total control over who can—and can't—
> view your profile data. See Lesson 2 for more information about
> editing your profile.

To delete your Google+ profile, follow these steps:

1. Click the **Home** icon on the Google+ ribbon and select **Settings**
   from the drop-down menu in the upper-right corner of the page
   (refer to Figure 5.1).

2. On the Google Accounts page, select the **Account** tab.

3. At the bottom of the Account tab, click the **Delete Profile and Remove Associated Google+ Features** link.

4. On the Delete Google+ Content or Your Entire Google Profile page, select the **Delete Google+ Content** option button to delete your profile content, including circles, posts, and comments, but retain a basic profile for use with Google products that use profile data. Optionally, select the **Delete Your Entire Google Profile** option button to delete circles, posts, comments, *and* your profile.

5. Check the box stating that you understand that deleting this service can't be undone and the data deleted can't be restored.

6. Click the **Remove Selected Services** button and confirm your deletion.

Deleting Your Google Account

Another option is to delete your entire Google account, which removes access to all Google products, including Google+.

CAUTION: **Think Twice Before Deleting Your Google Account**

Deleting your Google account doesn't just delete your Google+ profile. It also deletes your account on any other Google products you have, such as Gmail, Google Reader, Google Buzz, Google Checkout, and more. Be very sure that you really want to delete *everything* before proceeding with this option. If privacy is your concern, this lesson offers many suggestions for protecting your privacy while still maintaining your accounts.

To delete your Google account, follow these steps:

1. Click the **Home** icon on the Google+ ribbon and select **Settings** from the drop-down menu in the upper-right corner of the page (refer to Figure 5.1).

2. On the Google Accounts page, select the **Account** tab.

3. At the bottom of the Account tab, click the **Close Account and Delete All Services and Info Associated with It** link to open the Delete Google Account page. This is a powerful page; it enables you to delete your accounts for *all* Google products.

4. Select the check box next to each Google product that displays on this page. This confirms that you understand Google will delete your account on these products and you can no longer use them. You can't select only certain check boxes; you must select them all to confirm you really want to delete all Google products.

5. Confirm your password.

6. Confirm that you want to delete your account and that you understand that you're still responsible for any pending financial transactions (for example, using Google Wallet) by selecting the corresponding check boxes.

7. Click the **Delete Google Account** button and confirm the permanent deletion of your account.

Managing Your Security

To manage your Google security settings, click the **Home** icon on the Google+ ribbon, select **Settings** from the drop-down menu in the upper-right corner of the page (see Figure 5.1), and click the **Security** tab on the Google Accounts page.

On the Security tab, you can do the following:

▶ **Change your password.** Click the **Change Password** button to open the Change Password page. To create a secure password, use a combination of uppercase letters, lowercase letters, and numbers. For more password tips, click the Password Strength link on this page.

▶ **Change your recovery options.** Click the **Account Recovery Options** button to open the Account Recovery Options page. Recovery options enable you to access your account even if you forget your password. Options include password recovery by email, text message, or security question.

▶ **Enable 2-step verification.** Click the **Edit** link to the right of the 2-step Verification field to set up 2-step verification. This feature adds an extra layer of protection to your account but requires that you enter both a password and a verification code each time you sign in.

▶ **Authorize and revoke access to your account.** Click the **Edit** link to the right of the Authorizing Applications and Sites field to open the Authorized Access to Your Google Account page, shown in Figure 5.3. This page lists all the third-party applications you've authorized to access your Google account, such as Google+ games or other social sites. You can revoke access to any third-party application, but doing so means that your account will no longer be connected. For example, you can no longer play games to which you revoke access.

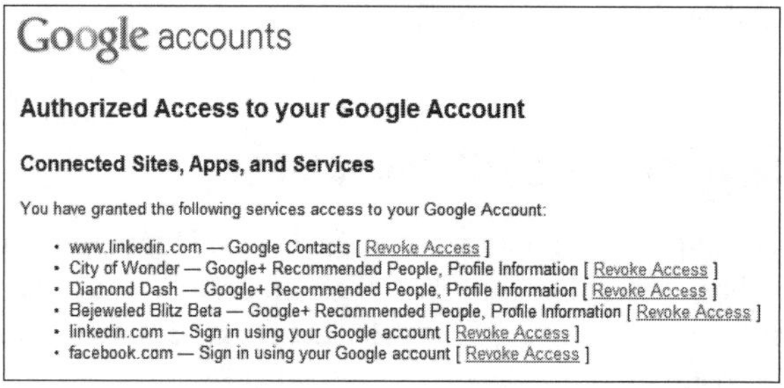

Google accounts

Authorized Access to your Google Account

Connected Sites, Apps, and Services

You have granted the following services access to your Google Account:

- www.linkedin.com — Google Contacts [Revoke Access]
- City of Wonder — Google+ Recommended People, Profile Information [Revoke Access]
- Diamond Dash — Google+ Recommended People, Profile Information [Revoke Access]
- Bejeweled Blitz Beta — Google+ Recommended People, Profile Information [Revoke Access]
- linkedin.com — Sign in using your Google account [Revoke Access]
- facebook.com — Sign in using your Google account [Revoke Access]

FIGURE 5.3   You can revoke access to any third-party applications.

Managing Your Privacy Settings

To manage your privacy settings, click the **Home** icon on the Google+ ribbon, select **Settings** from the drop-down menu in the upper-right corner of the page (refer to Figure 5.1), and click the **Profile and Privacy** tab on the Google Accounts page.

Managing Privacy Settings for Your Google+ Profile

The Google Profiles section on the Profile and Privacy tab previews what your Google+ profile looks like in search results, as shown in Figure 5.4.

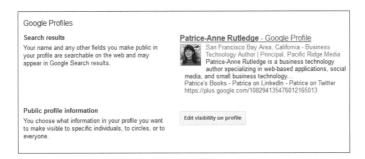

FIGURE 5.4   Manage your profile visibility.

To edit your profile visibility, click the **Edit Visibility on Profile** button to open your profile in Edit mode. For example, you can specify privacy settings for each section of your profile and choose whether to make your profile visible in search engine results. See Lesson 2 for more information about editing your profile.

Managing Google+ Sharing

The Sharing section of the Profile and Privacy page, shown in Figure 5.5, helps you manage the privacy of the content you share on Google+.

This section provides information about Google+ sharing all in one place with tips, information, and links to other areas of Google+ where you can specify your sharing preferences. In this section, you can:

▶ Click the **Manage Circles** button to open the Circles page where you can place people in circles that determine what content they can view. See Lesson 4, "Managing Your Network with Circles," for more information about how circles help you manage the way you share with others.

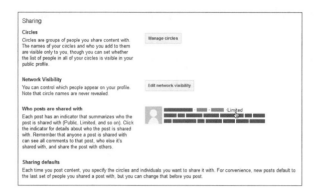

FIGURE 5.5   Learn more about how sharing works in Google+.

▶ Click the **Edit Network Visibility** button to open the About tab on your profile where you can disable search engine visibility if you don't want anyone to find your profile on a search engine such as Google, Yahoo!, or Bing (using the Profile Discovery field). See Lesson 2 for more information about profile privacy.

Managing Other Google+ Privacy Options

The remaining buttons on the Profile and Privacy tab enable you to establish additional privacy settings. Here, you can do the following:

▶ Click the **Edit Photos Settings** button to open the Photos section of the Google+ tab where you can manage your photo settings. See Lesson 10, "Working with Photos," for more information.

▶ Click the **Sign into Dashboard** button to sign in to your Google Dashboard. On the Dashboard, you can manage all your Google products, including Google+, Gmail, Docs, Talk, Buzz, and more.

▶ Click the **Go to Privacy Center** button to open the Google Privacy Center page, which includes information and videos about protecting your privacy.

Managing Google+ Settings

To manage your Google+ settings, click the **Home** icon on the Google+ ribbon, select **Settings** from the drop-down menu in the upper-right corner of the page (refer to Figure 5.1), and click the **Google+** tab on the Google Accounts page. Figure 5.6 shows the Google+ tab.

FIGURE 5.6   Specify how you want Google+ to notify you on the Google+ tab.

On this tab, you can set your email and phone delivery preferences, set your notification preferences, and specify +1 personalization.

This tab also offers several fields for specifying photo preferences. See Lesson 10 for more information about these preferences.

Specifying Who Can Interact with You and Your Posts

The Who Can Interact with You and Your Posts section enables you to control exactly who can send you notifications and comment on your public posts. Your choices include Anyone, Extended Circles, Your Circles,

Only You, or Custom (this gives you the option of selecting specific circles or people). By default, Google+ allows people in your extended circles to send you notifications and allows anyone to comment on your public posts.

Setting Notification Delivery Preferences

The Notification Delivery section of the Google+ tab displays the email address and mobile phone number where you want to receive notifications. You can change your email address on the Account Overview tab. If you haven't connected a mobile phone to this account, you can do so on this tab. To learn more about how Google+ notifications work, see Lesson 9, "Viewing and Managing Notifications."

To add a phone number, follow these steps:

1. Click the **Add Phone Number** link in the Notification Delivery section of the Google+ tab.

2. Enter your country and phone number.

3. Click the **Send Verification Code** button. Google+ sends a verification code by text message to your phone.

4. Enter your six-digit code in the Verification Code field and click the **Confirm** button.

5. Select the **SMS** option button if you want to receive selected Google+ notifications by text message. Select the **Don't Notify Me** option button if you don't want to receive text message notifications.

Be sure to specify your notification preferences after enabling SMS so that you can control the volume of messages you receive.

Managing Email Subscriptions

By default, Google+ sends you occasional updates about top content from your circles, Google+ activity, and friend suggestions. If you don't want to receive these updates, remove the check marks in the Manage Email Subscriptions section.

Specifying Notification Preferences

The Receive Notifications section of the Google+ tab enables you to specify which actions trigger a Google+ notification and how to send this notification: by email, via SMS text message, or both.

Figure 5.7 shows the Receive Notifications section, which displays the events that trigger notifications, such as when someone mentions you in a post, adds you to a circle, tags you, comments on one of your posts, starts a Messenger conversation with you, and so forth.

FIGURE 5.7 You have control over which notifications you receive and how you receive them.

For each event, you can select your preferred notification method. If you don't want to receive any notifications, remove the check marks from all check boxes.

> **NOTE: Why Can't I Select the Phone Check Box?**
>
> You must select the SMS option button in the Notification Delivery section at the top of this tab to activate the Phone column.

Enabling +1 Personalization

By default, Google+ disables +1 personalization on third-party sites, but you can enable this feature if you want to. When you enable +1 personalization, Google uses your account data, such as the names of people in your circles, to personalize content and ads on third-party sites. For example, you could see the name of someone in one of your circles who has clicked the +1 button to show support for a post on a popular website.

To enable this feature, follow these steps:

1. Click the **Edit** link in the Google +1 section on the Google+ tab.

2. On the +1 Personalization on Non-Google Sites page, shown in Figure 5.8, select the **Enable** option button. If you want to read more information about the ramifications of this choice, click the **Learn More** link to open a page with a detailed explanation of +1 personalization with several examples.

FIGURE 5.8   Decide whether you want to enable +1 personalization.

3. Click the **Save** button.

Adding Google+ Pages to Your Circles

If you search for a Google+ page on Google by inserting the plus sign (+) before the page name (such as "+Toyota"), Google can add this page automatically to your circles. To activate this feature, select the check box in the Google+ Pages section.

Displaying Content About Google+ Games

By default, Google+ displays links to recently played games on the side of your stream and shows Google+ game notifications on the Notifications menu. To disable either of these features, remove the check marks from the associated check boxes.

Customizing Your Circles

By default, when you choose to share content with Your Circles, Google+ shares with all your circles except the Following circle. To customize this, click the **Customize** button in the Your Circles section. In the pop-up box that opens, you can select the specific circles you want to include in Your Circles.

Managing Google+ Photo Settings

Optionally, Google+ enables you to:

▶ Show your photos' geographic location in newly uploaded albums and photos.

▶ Allow viewers to download your photos.

▶ Find your face in photos, prompt people in your circles to tag you, and specify whose tags to approve automatically.

To enable any of these options, place a check mark in the associated check box.

Managing Your Products

To manage Google products other than Google+, click the **Home** icon on the Google+ ribbon, select **Settings** from the drop-down menu in the upper-right corner of the page (refer to Figure 5.1), and click the **Products** tab on the Google Accounts page.

On the Your Products page, you can manage your settings for other Google products you use, including Alerts, Docs, Gmail, Google Music, Knol, Picasa Web Albums, Talk, Voice, YouTube, AdSense, AdWords, and more.

Specifying Your Preferred Languages

Google enables you to view its products in multiple languages. For example, you can view Google+ in more than 40 languages, ranging from Arabic to Vietnamese. Because Google hasn't localized all its products in every language it supports, you can specify secondary languages if your primary language isn't available for a specific product.

To specify your preferred languages, follow these steps:

1. Click the **Settings** link in the upper-right corner of any Google+ page. Click the **Home** icon on the Google+ ribbon and select **Settings** from the drop-down menu in the upper-right corner of the page (refer to Figure 5.1).

2. Click the **Language** tab on the Google Accounts page.

3. Select your default language from the Primary Language drop-down list (see Figure 5.9). This field displays the current language you're using to view the Google+ interface, but you can choose from dozens of other languages. For example, if you're currently viewing Google+ in English but would rather view it in Italian, select Italian as your primary language.

FIGURE 5.9   View Google+ in your preferred language.

4. If you changed your default language in step 3, click the **Reload** link to switch languages. Figure 5.10 shows Google+ in Italian. Be aware that although Google localizes the Google+ product interface, user content such as posts and comments remain in their original language.

FIGURE 5.10 Google+ is available in more than 40 languages, including Italian.

5. Optionally, click the **Add Another Language** link to add a second language to this list. This option is useful if you would like to view Google products in another language you know when your native language isn't available. For example, if you're a native speaker of Estonian but also speak English, you should list Estonian first and then English.

You can change a secondary language to your primary language by clicking the **Make Primary** link to its right. You can also delete a language by clicking the **Remove** link to its right. You can change your primary language, but you can't delete it.

Backing Up Your Data

Google enables you to back up your critical data using Google Takeout, which creates a downloadable archive of your +1s, Buzz content, contacts, Picasa Web Albums, and Google+ profile, circles, and stream. You can download all your Google data or only specific data.

To download your Google data, follow these steps:

1. Click the **Home** icon on the Google+ ribbon and select **Settings** from the drop-down menu in the upper-right corner of the page (refer to Figure 5.1).

2. On the Google Accounts page, select the **Data Liberation** tab, as shown in Figure 5.11.

3. Click the **Download Your Data** button. Optionally, you can click one of the five links that display at the bottom of the page to download only specific data.

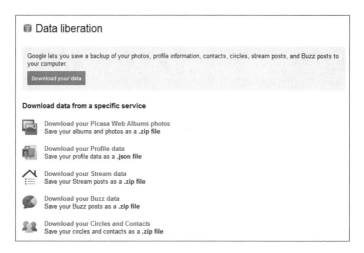

FIGURE 5.11   Back up your Google+ data for safekeeping.

4. Confirm your password to verify your identity.

5. On the Takeout page, click the **All of Your Data** tab. Optionally, click the **Choose Services** tab and select from the available download options: +1s, Buzz, Circles, Contacts, Knol, Picasa Web Albums, Profile, Stream, or Voice.

6. Click the **Create Archive** button. Google+ analyzes your data and displays a summary on the Downloads tab, as shown in Figure 5.12. Your download is available for one week.

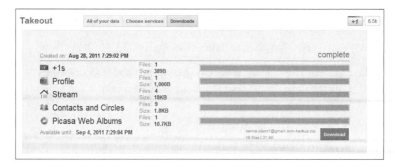

FIGURE 5.12   The Downloads tab summarizes your data archive.

7. Click the **Download** button in the lower-right corner. Google prompts you to save your download file to your computer. The exact process for this varies by operating system and browser.

Google places a .zip file in your default Downloads folder, or in a folder you specify, using the following naming convention: [email address]-backup.zip. You can store this file for safekeeping or unzip it for another use, such as managing downloaded photos in an external photo album.

Summary

In this lesson, you learned how to manage your Google+ account and privacy settings. Next, you can get started sharing some content on Google+.

LESSON 6

Sharing Content on Google+

In this lesson, you learn how to share content on Google+, including photos, videos, and links.

Using the Share Box

The share box displays at the top of your Google+ home page, ready for you to share interesting content with your friends and colleagues—or everyone on the Web. Using the share box, you can share text updates, links, photos, and videos.

To share a post using the share box, follow these steps:

1. Click the **Home** icon on the Google+ ribbon, if you aren't already on your home page. Figure 6.1 displays the share box on your Google+ stream, which opens. Your stream enables you to share content as well as view content other people have shared. See Lesson 7, "Viewing Your Google+ Stream," for more information.

FIGURE 6.1   Click the Home icon to access the share box on your Google+ stream.

2. Click in the share box to expand it, as shown in Figure 6.2. Alternately, click the **Share** button that displays in the upper-right corner of any Google+ page to access the share box.

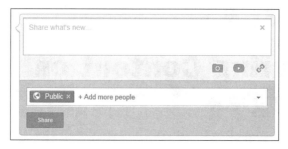

FIGURE 6.2 Expand the share box to display additional fields.

3. Type your post in the text box.

4. Optionally, you can add other content and apply formatting to your posts. These tasks are covered later in this lesson. For example, you can do the following:

   ▶ Format your post using bolding and italics.

   ▶ Add a link to the profile of another Google+ user you mention.

   ▶ Add a photo.

   ▶ Add a video.

   ▶ Add a link to an external website.

5. Specify who you want to share this post with. Your options include the following:

   ▶ **Anyone on the Web.** By default, Google+ makes your initial post public, visible to anyone on the Web. Later, Google+ uses the default settings from your most recent post. If you don't want to share this post publicly, click the **Delete** icon (x) on the right side of the Public chip.

   ▶ **People in specific circles.** To share this post with specific circles, click the **Add More People** link. In the menu that opens (see Figure 6.3), select the circles you want to share with. If you want to share with all your circles, select **Your Circles**. If you want to share with your extended circles (friends of friends), select **Extended Circles**. When you're finished selecting circles, click outside the menu to close it.

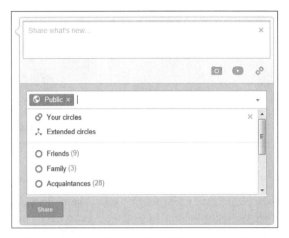

FIGURE 6.3   You can choose the specific circles you want to share with.

▶ **A specific person.** This is the equivalent of sending a private message on Google+. If the person you want to share with uses Google+, type the person's name in the text box and select from the pop-up menu of potential matches (see Figure 6.4). Optionally, you can enter an email address to share with someone who doesn't use Google+ yet.

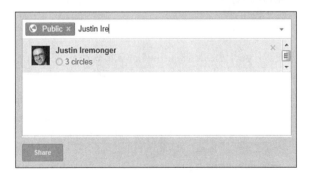

FIGURE 6.4   You can share a post with just one person.

NOTE: **Understanding Color-Coded Sharing Chips**

Google+ uses color-coded chips to differentiate the groups of people you share with. The Public and Extended Circles chips are green, which signifies that you are sharing with people you don't know. The chips corresponding to your own circles or individual people are blue, which signifies that you are sharing with people you know.

6. If you want to send a notification and email message about this post to the people in a circle, hover the mouse above that circle and select the **Notify About This Post** check box. In general, you should send notifications and emails only for very urgent or important posts.

7. If any of the people in your selected circles aren't on Google+ yet, click the following link to send them your post by email instead: **Also Email [Number of] People Not Yet Using Google+**. For example, if two people you added to circles haven't signed up for Google+ yet, this link says "2 People." Again, use caution when emailing people and send emails only for very important content.

NOTE: **Who Will Receive an Email?**

To view a list of the people who will receive this email, click the **[Number of] People** link. A pop-up box displays the people in your circles who aren't on Google+ yet.

8. Optionally, click the down arrow in the lower-right corner of the share box and choose one or both of the following options:

   ▶ **Disable Comments.** Prevent others from commenting on your post. This is most useful if your posts receive comment spam. Users will still be able to reshare your post and click the +1 button to support it. Click the **Okay, Got It** button to activate this feature. If you change your mind, click the down arrow again and select **Enable Comments** from the menu.

> ▶ **Lock This Post.** Prevent others from resharing your post
> or mentioning people you haven't shared with. Click the
> **Okay, Lock It** button to activate this feature. A lock icon
> displays in the lower-right corner of the share box. If you
> change your mind, click the down arrow again and select
> **Unlock This Post** from the menu.

9. Click the **Share** button to share your post with the people you
selected.

Figure 6.5 shows a sample post, visible on the streams of the people you
shared with as well as on your public profile if you selected to make this
post public.

Patrice-Anne Rutledge 2:23 PM · Limited
Some days it's just nice to escape the office, even if you work from home.

+1   ↱   ▣◀

Add a comment...

FIGURE 6.5   A post shared on Google+.

After you share a post:

> ▶ You can edit its content, delete it, or prevent others from sharing
> or commenting on it.

> ▶ Your Google+ network can comment on, share, or +1 this post.

See Lesson 7 for more information about these tasks and features.

Formatting Your Posts

Google+ enables you to format your posts using bolding, italics, and strikethroughs. You can do the following:

- ▶ Bold text by surrounding it with asterisks.
- ▶ Italicize text by surrounding it with underscores.
- ▶ Strike through text by surrounding it with hyphens.

Figure 6.6 shows an example of formatting text in the share box.

FIGURE 6.6   Use these characters to apply text formatting to your posts.

Figure 6.7 shows an example of the results of this formatting.

FIGURE 6.7   Formatting in a live post.

Mentioning Other People in Your Posts

When you mention another Google+ user in a post, you can link to that person's Google+ profile. Mentioning a person is most useful when you want to give someone public credit or thanks within the Google+ community. Google+ also notifies this person of the mention.

To mention someone in a post, enter the plus sign (+) or at sign (@) in the share box, start typing someone's name, and select the person you want to mention, as shown in Figure 6.8.

FIGURE 6.8   Select the person you want to mention from the list of Google+ users.

Figure 6.9 shows a sample mention in a published post. You can pause your mouse over a mention to view a pop-up box with more information or click the mentioned name to view this person's Google+ profile.

FIGURE 6.9   Pause your mouse over a mention to view a pop-up box.

Sharing Photos

You can easily share photos on your Google+ posts. For example, you could share vacation photos only with your Friends and Family circles or photos of your company's products on a public post. Google+ offers unlimited photo uploads. If your photos are larger than 2,048 by 2,048 pixels, however, Google+ resizes them during the upload process.

See Lesson 10, "Working with Photos," for more information about the many ways you can use photos in Google+.

To share a photo on Google+, follow these steps:

1. Click the **Home** icon on the Google+ ribbon if you aren't already on your home page (refer to Figure 6.1).

2. Click in the share box to expand it (refer to Figure 6.2). Alternately, click the **Share** button that displays in the upper-right corner of any Google+ page to access the share box.

3. Type your post in the text box. For example, you can introduce or comment on the photo you're sharing.

4. Click the **Add Photos** button in the lower-right corner of the share box. A pop-up menu opens, offering three ways to add photos (see Figure 6.10).

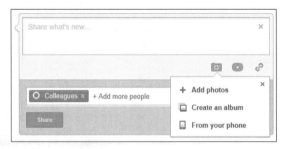

FIGURE 6.10   Add photos to enliven your posts.

5. Attach your photo to the post by selecting one of the following menu options:

▶ **Add Photos.** Search for and upload photos from your computer. After adding photos (see Figure 6.11), you can click the

> ▶ **Edit Photos** link to add captions, rotate your photos, or open Picnick to access advanced photo editing features.

> ▶ **Tag People** link to add tags to photos that include people.

> ▶ **Add Text** link to overlay text on your photos.

> ▶ **Add More** link to upload additional photos.

> ▶ **Remove All** link to remove all formatting.

> ▶ **Remove** button (x) to delete the photos you added.

FIGURE 6.11   You can edit your photo or add more photos to your post.

▶ **Create an Album.** Create and upload a photo album by selecting multiple photos from your computer. See Lesson 10 for more information about photo albums.

▶ **From Your Phone.** Upload photos from your phone. You must have an iPhone or Android smartphone and download the Google+ app to use this feature. Google+ uploads the photos you take from your phone and places them on the Photos from Your Phone tab on the Photos page. These photos remain private until you choose to share them. See Lesson 10 for more information about uploading photos from your phone.

6. Select the people or circles you want to share this post with or, optionally, make this post public. For a reminder of how to do this, refer to steps 5 through 7 in the section "Using the Share Box" earlier in this lesson.

7. Click the **Share** button to share your post with the people you selected.

Figure 6.12 shows a sample post with a photo.

FIGURE 6.12   A shared post that appears on your stream.

After posting your photo, you can click it to use the lightbox view, where you can edit it, add a caption, add tags, and more. See Lesson 10 for more information about working with photos.

Sharing Videos

Sharing videos is another way to enliven your posts. Google+ gives you three ways to share your videos. You can upload from your phone, share from YouTube, or upload from your Android 2.1+ smartphone. Google+ lets you upload an unlimited number of videos of up to 15 minutes each.

To share a video on Google+, follow these steps:

1. Click the **Home** icon on the Google+ ribbon if you aren't already on your home page (refer to Figure 6.1).

2. Click in the share box to expand it (refer to Figure 6.2). Alternately, click the **Share** button that displays in the upper-right corner of any Google+ page to access the share box.

3. Type your post in the text box. For example, you can introduce or comment on the video you're sharing.

4. Click the **Add Video** button in the lower-right corner of the share box. A pop-up menu opens, offering four ways to add videos (see Figure 6.13).

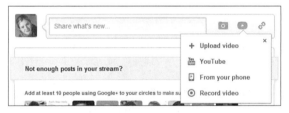

FIGURE 6.13   Google+ gives you four ways to add videos.

5. Attach your video to the post by selecting one of the following menu options:

   ▶ **Upload Video.** Open the Upload Videos dialog box from which you can upload videos from your computer. Select the videos you want to upload and click the **Add Videos** button.

▶ **YouTube.** Search for YouTube videos by keyword, enter
the URL of a specific YouTube video, or select from
YouTube videos you've shared in the past. Figure 6.14
shows the Choose a YouTube Video dialog box from
which you select your video.

FIGURE 6.14   Embed a YouTube video on a Google+ post.

▶ **From Your Phone.** Upload videos from your phone. You
must have an iPhone or Android smartphone and download
the Google+ app to use this feature.

▶ **Record Video.** Record a video from your webcam.

6. Select the people or circles you want to share this post with or,
optionally, make this post public. For a reminder of how to do
this, refer to steps 5 through 7 in the section "Using the Share
Box" earlier in this lesson.

7. Click the **Share** button to share your post with the people you
selected. Users can click the Play button in any embedded video
to play it directly on Google+.

Sharing Links

Google+ makes it easy to share links to external websites in your posts. For example, you might want to share your latest blog post or an interesting article you read on the Web.

To share a link on Google+, follow these steps:

1. Click the **Home** icon the Google+ ribbon if you aren't already on your home page.

2. Click in the share box to expand it (refer to Figure 6.2). Alternately, click the **Share** button that displays in the upper-right corner of any Google+ page to access the share box.

3. Type your post in the text box. For example, you can introduce or comment on the link you're sharing.

4. Click the **Add Link** button in the lower-right corner of the share box, as shown in Figure 6.15. The share box expands to display new fields.

FIGURE 6.15   Link to an interesting website or blog post.

5. Enter the complete URL of the website page you want to link to, such as www.patricerutledge.com. Optionally, you can copy and paste a longer URL.

6. Click the **Add** button. The share box displays the link name, its description, and an image (if available), as shown in Figure 6.16.

FIGURE 6.16   Preview your link before posting.

NOTE: **Where Does Google+ Get the Link Data?**

Google+ retrieves the link name, description, and image from the metadata and content on the site you're linking to. Optionally, you can delete the default description by clicking the **Remove Description** link or delete the default image by clicking the **Delete** button (small x) in the upper-right corner of the image.

---

7. Select the people or circles you want to share this post with or, optionally, make this post public. For a reminder of how to do this, refer to steps 5 through 7 in the section "Using the Share Box" earlier in this lesson.

8. Click the **Share** button to share your post with the people you selected.

Figure 6.17 shows a sample posted link, visible on the streams of the people you shared with as well as on your public profile if you selected to make this post public.

FIGURE 6.17 Click a link to visit the shared site.

Summary

In this lesson, you learned how to post content on Google+. Next, you learn how to view and manage your Google+ stream.

LESSON 7

Viewing Your Google+ Stream

In this lesson, you learn how to view, manage, and participate in your Google+ stream.

Exploring Your Stream

On Google+, the center of activity is your stream. This is the first page you see when you sign into Google+ and the place where you'll spend the majority of your time on the site.

PLAIN ENGLISH: **Google+ Stream**

The Google+ stream offers a central location for viewing the posts, links, photos, and videos that you and others have shared. You can join the conversation on the stream by adding your own posts and comments, sharing interesting content you discover, and supporting quality posts using the Google +1 button.

Your Google+ stream, shown in Figure 7.1, displays the posts submitted by people in your circles, your posts, and selected Hot on Google+ posts (trending content across Google+ that Google deems particularly interesting or informative). See "Viewing the Explore Page" later in this lesson to learn more about Hot on Google+ posts and how you can control how many of them display in your stream.

If you have only a few people in your circles, Google+ displays the Not Enough People in Your Stream? section, which helps you find more people to add.

FIGURE 7.1   Your stream is the center of activity on Google+.

Accessing Your Stream

Your Google+ stream isn't hard to find. It's the first page you see when you sign into Google+. If you go to another location on Google+, you can return to your stream by clicking the **Home** icon on the Google+ ribbon.

Viewing a Sample Post

Figure 7.2 shows a sample Google+ post shared by someone in one of your circles.

For each post, you can do the following:

▶ Pause your mouse over someone's name to view a pop-up with more information about this person.

▶ Click someone's name to view this person's Google+ profile.

▶ Click the date to view other posts from that date.

+1 this post   Start a hangout

Share this post

FIGURE 7.2   Viewing a basic post in your Google+ stream.

▶ Click the **Limited** link to view gravatars of people the post author shared with. The **Limited** link displays only when the author shared this content with specific circles rather than publicly. If the **Public** link displays instead, the author shared the content publicly and it's visible to anyone on the Web.

▶ Click the **+1 This Post** button to show your support for this post using Google +1. See "Liking a Post Using the +1 Button" later in this lesson for more information.

▶ Click the **Share This Post** button to share this post with others. See "Sharing Posts" later in this lesson for more information.

▶ Click the **Start a Hangout About This Post** button to start a hangout with the post author. See Lesson 12, "Using Hangouts for Video Chat," to learn more about hangouts.

▶ Click the **Add a Comment** box to add a comment. See "Commenting on Posts" later in this lesson for more information.

Depending on the actions of the original author and the people reading the post, other content might be available. Figure 7.3 shows a post with additional content and conversation.

FIGURE 7.3 Viewing a post with lots of conversation.

When a post contains additional content or activity, other options for interaction become available. For example, you can

▶ Click a link to view content from an external site, such as a blog post that someone shared on Google+.

▶ Click an attached photo to enlarge it or add tags to it. See Lesson 10, "Working with Photos," for more information about tagging photos.

▶ Click a video to play it in Google+.

▶ Pause your mouse over the name of someone mentioned in a post to view a pop-up box with more information about this person. Optionally, click the person's name to view this person's profile. Google+ identifies a mention by placing the plus sign (+) before someone's name, such as +Anne Smith.

▶ View the number of +1's. Click the **+[number]** link to view a complete list of people who shared. For example, if 8 people shared this post, the link name would be +8.

▶ View the number of shares, including the names of some people who shared this post. Click the **[Number] Shares** link to view a complete list of people who shared. For example, if 12 people shared this post, the link name would be 12 Shares.

▶ View the most recent comments at the end of a post. To view additional comments, click the **[Number] Comments** link. Click the **Expand This Comment** link to view the entire text of longer comments. You can also add your own comment to an existing comment. See "Commenting on Posts" later in this lesson for more information.

Be aware that all of these options might not be available for every post. For example, not all posts contain links, videos, photos, mentions, comments, shares, and +1's.

Filtering Your Stream

By default, Google+ displays both your posts and the posts of people in your circles on your stream. If you have a large network with many circles, however, your stream can become overloaded with too much content.

To filter your stream, click the name of a circle above the share box (see Figure 7.4). By default, the Friends and Family circles display here. To access other circles, click the **More** button and select a circle from the drop-down menu.

FIGURE 7.4   You can filter your stream by circle.

Google+ displays only the posts from the people in this circle. For example, if you click the **Friends** button, your stream displays only posts from people in this circle.

If you want to view only your own posts, click the **Profile** icon on the Google+ ribbon. All your posts display on the Posts tab of your profile.

NOTE: **Why Did My Content Disappear When I Applied a Filter?**

Be aware that if no one in a circle has posted on Google+, you won't see any content when you filter to that circle. This is particularly common if you have only a few people in a circle and they are new to Google+.

TIP: **Google+ Displays Game-Related Posts on the Games Stream**

If you enjoy playing games, Google+ displays all posts related to your gaming activities on the Games stream and not on the main Google+ stream. This way, only your game buddies need to know about your high score on Bejeweled Blitz or your other game achievements. See Lesson 13, "Playing Games," for more information about Google+ games and the Games stream.

Participating in the Stream

After you've spent some time reading posts in your stream, you'll probably want to join the conversation and start adding your own commentary. Google+ gives you the option to show your support for a post with +1, add a comment to a post, or share a post.

Liking a Post Using the +1 Button

One of the fastest and easiest ways to let people know that you like specific content in your Google+ stream is to use the +1 button.

PLAIN ENGLISH: **Google +1 Button**

The **Google +1 button** offers a way to publicly show your support for a post that you like. The +1 button is available on Google+ and, optionally, on other websites and blogs that choose to enable this button. Google+ uses the term "+1" as both a noun and verb. In other words, you +1 a post using the +1 button. To learn more about the concept behind the Google +1 button, visit www.google.com/+1/button.

If you want to show others that you like a post in your stream, click the **+1** button that displays below the post content (see Figure 7.5).

FIGURE 7.5 Click the +1 button to show your support for a post.

Your stream shows that you +1'd the post (see Figure 7.6). Be aware that this action is public and others can also see that you +1'd the post.

FIGURE 7.6 You can see the posts you +1'd in your stream.

If you clicked the +1 button by mistake, click it again (it's now red) to undo your +1.

TIP: **Show Your Support for a Comment Using the +1 Button**

Using the +1 button isn't reserved for posts; you can use it to support comments as well. If you want to show your support for a particularly interesting or insightful comment, pause your mouse over it and click the +1 button to its right.

Commenting on Posts

If you have something to say about a post, you can add your own commentary.

To add a comment, follow these steps:

1. Click the **Add a Comment** link at the bottom of the post you want to comment on.

2. Type your comment in the text box that displays (see Figure 7.7).

FIGURE 7.7 Join the conversation on Google+ by adding your own comments.

3. Click the **Post Comment** button to post your comment. Figure 7.8 shows a sample published comment.

FIGURE 7.8 Your comment displays at the end of a post.

TIP: **Apply Styles and Mention People in a Comment**

Just like with a post, you can apply styles such as bolding and italics to your comment text. You can also mention other Google+ users and include a link to their profiles. See Lesson 6, "Sharing Content on Google+," for more information about applying styles and mentioning other Google+ users.

Editing a Comment

After posting a comment, you might notice a typo or think of something else you want to add.

To edit a comment you wrote, follow these steps:

1. Click the **Edit** link to the right of the comment.

2. Make your changes in the text box.

3. Click the **Save Changes** button.

Google+ updates your comment with the changes you made.

Deleting a Comment

If you decide that posting your comment wasn't such a good idea after all, you can delete it.

To delete a comment you wrote, click the **Edit** link to the right of the comment and then click the **Delete Comment** button.

Google+ permanently deletes your comment.

Sharing Posts

When you find an interesting post on Google+, you can share it with others. You can also share post comments.

To share a post, follow these steps:

1. Click the **Share This Post** button below the post you want to share, as shown in Figure 7.9.

Share this post

FIGURE 7.9   Share interesting posts with others on Google+.

CAUTION: **Consider Carefully Who You Share With**

If the original author shared this post only with a limited audience (such as people in circles), Google+ reminds you of this fact and encourages you to use discretion when sharing. In general, it's good etiquette to focus on sharing posts that others made public rather than only with those in their chosen circles.

2. In the Share This Post box, shown in Figure 7.10, add your own comments about the post in the text box.

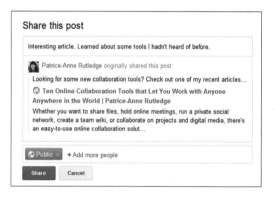

FIGURE 7.10   Add your own comments to the content you share.

3. If the original author made this post public, Google+ makes your shared version public as well, visible to anyone on the Web. If you don't want to share this post publicly, click the **Delete** icon (x) on the right side of the Public button. If the original author shared this post only with a limited audience, you can share it with your circles but not publicly.

4. To share this post with specific circles, click the **Add More People** link.

5. In the menu that opens (see Figure 7.11), select the circles you want to share with. If you want to share with all your circles, select **Your Circles.** If you want to share with your extended circles (friends of friends), select **Extended Circles**.

FIGURE 7.11   You can choose the specific circles you want to share with.

6. When you're finished selecting circles, click outside the menu to close it.

7. If you want to send a notification and email about this post to the people in a circle, hover the mouse above that circle and select the **Notify About This Post** check box. In general, you should send notifications and emails only for very urgent or important posts.

8. If any of the people in your selected circles aren't on Google+ yet, you have the option to send them an email about this post. To do so, click the **Also Email [Number of] People Not Yet Using Google+** check box. To view the people who will receive this email, click the **[Number of] People** link. For example, if two people you added to circles haven't signed up for Google+ yet, this link says "2 People." Again, use caution when emailing people and send emails only for very important content.

9. Click the **Share** button to share your post with the people you selected.

Figure 7.12 shows a sample shared post, visible on the streams of the people you shared with as well as on your public profile if you selected to make this post public. Your Google+ network can comment on, share, or +1 any post you share.

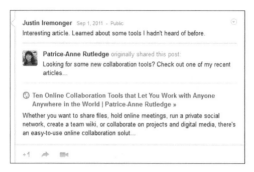

FIGURE 7.12   A shared post that appears on your stream.

> NOTE: **Google+ Ripples Illustrates the Impact of Sharing**
> When you—or anyone else—shares a post, Google+ displays this
> action in graphic format through Google+ Ripples. To view a ripple
> diagram for a post that's been shared, click the down arrow in the
> upper-right corner of the post and select **View Ripples** from the
> menu. A diagram opens that displays the people who shared the
> post and their connection to others who shared. Be aware that a
> ripple diagram displays data only for the past 53 days.

Managing Your Posts in the Stream

After you share posts to the Google+ stream, you might want to make a
few changes. To manage a post you created, click the small down arrow in
the upper-right corner of the post to open the Options menu. By selecting
an option from this menu, you can edit a post, delete a post, report or
remove comments, disable comments, or lock a post. This menu displays
only for your own posts. See "Managing Your Circles' Posts in the
Stream" later in this lesson to learn about the menu options available for
posts from people in your circles.

> TIP: **View All Your Posts on Your Profile**
>
> If you want to view only your own posts rather than the mixed assortment of posts that display on your stream, you can do so on the Posts tab of your profile. The Options menu is available there as well.

Editing a Post

For example, you can edit a post to fix a typo; to add a photo, video, or link you forgot to include; or delete something you regret posting.

To edit one of your posts, follow these steps:

1. Click the down arrow in the upper-right corner of your post to open the Options menu, as shown in Figure 7.13.

FIGURE 7.13 If you make a mistake, you can edit your post.

> CAUTION: **Post Edits Don't Transfer to Shared Content**
>
> If someone shared your post before you edited it, the original version of the post will remain in any shared locations. If a post contains a serious error that needs to be changed, you must ask the people who shared to delete and share again.

Deleting a Post

To delete one of your posts, follow these steps:

1. Click the down arrow in the upper-right corner of your post.

2. Select **Delete This Post** from the Options menu (refer to Figure 7.13).

3. Click the **Delete** button in the dialog box that opens to confirm the deletion. Google+ permanently removes the post from your stream. You can no longer view this post nor can anyone you shared it with.

CAUTION: **Deleting Doesn't Remove Shared Posts**

If someone shared your post before you deleted it, the shared version of the post will remain on Google+. To delete the shared versions of your posts, you must ask the people who shared to delete as well. If you don't want people to be able to share a post, you should lock it. See "Locking a Post" later in this lesson for more information.

Disabling Comments

If you don't want people to comment on a post, you can disable comments for it.

To disable comments for a post, click the down arrow in the upper-right corner of the post and select **Disable Comments** from the Options menu (refer to Figure 7.13).

Google+ removes the Add a Comment link at the bottom of the post but retains any existing comments. Optionally, you can also remove any existing comments. See "Reporting or Removing Comments" later in this lesson for more information.

If you want to enable comments again, click the down arrow in the upper-right corner of the post and select **Enable Comments** from the Options menu.

Locking a Post

If you want to prevent others from sharing a post, you can lock it.

To lock a post, click the down arrow in the upper-right corner of your post and select **Lock This Post** from the Options menu (refer to Figure 7.13). Google+ alerts you that people can no longer share this post and removes the Share link at the bottom of the post.

If you want to unlock a post, click the down arrow in the upper-right corner of the post and select **Unlock This Post** from the Options menu.

Reporting or Deleting Comments

If others have commented on your post, you can report or delete any comment.

Reporting a Comment

If someone posts an inappropriate comment in response to one of your posts, you can report it to Google.

> CAUTION: **Consider Carefully Which Comments to Report as Abuse**
>
> You can report comments that violate Google+ terms and conditions (spam, nudity, hate speech, violence, copyright abuse, or child abuse). If someone simply disagrees with your post, you can remove the comment. Comments with dissenting opinions don't constitute abuse unless someone repeatedly posts comments to the point of harassment.

To report a comment, pause your mouse over it and click the **Report Abuse or Block** button (a small flag icon) to the right of the comment, as shown in Figure 7.14.

From here, you can pause your mouse over the Alert icon (grey triangle with an exclamation point) and click one of the following links:

▶ **Remove**, to remove the comment

▶ **Restore**, to restore the comment if you clicked the Report Abuse or Block button by mistake

▶ **Remove and Block This Person**, to remove the comment and
block this person from commenting again

Report Abuse or Block button

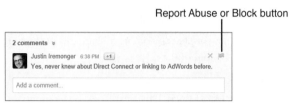

FIGURE 7.14   Click the flag icon to report abuse.

Google+ reviews all reports of abuse and takes appropriate action if
necessary.

Deleting a Comment

If you find an inappropriate or annoying comment on one of your posts,
you can delete it. To delete a comment, pause your mouse over it and click
the **Delete Comment** button (x) to its right (refer to Figure 7.14).

In the pop-up box that opens, click one of the following buttons: **Delete
Comment and Block This Person** or **Delete**. Google+ deletes the comment from your post.

When you block people, Google+ removes them from your circles and
extended circles, and their posts no longer display on your stream. In addition, they can't comment on your content posted after you blocked them or
mention you in their posts or comments. Be aware, however, that blocked
people can still view your public content on Google+ and can place you in
their own circles.

CAUTION: **Consider Other Options Before Blocking Someone**

Blocking is a strong action that should be reserved for those people who are posting inappropriate content or are harassing you on
Google+. You should consider other options before choosing to
block someone. For example, you can remove people from your circles if you no longer want to view their content. Or, if you just don't
want to see a specific post anymore, you can mute it.

Managing Your Circles' Posts in the Stream

Google+ also enables you to manage the content the people in your circles post. To manage a post of someone in one of your circles, click the small down arrow in the upper-right corner of the post to open the Options menu. By selecting an option from this menu, you can link to a post, report abuse, mute a post, or block the person who posted. This menu displays only for posts the people in your circles create. See "Managing Your Posts in the Stream" earlier in this lesson to learn about the menu options available for posts you create.

Linking to a Post

You can link to a public Google+ post from an external website or blog.

To link to a Google+ post, follow these steps:

1. Click the down arrow in the upper-right corner of the post (see Figure 7.15).

2. Select **Link to This Post** from the Options menu. Google+ opens the Link to This Post dialog box (see Figure 7.16).

3. Copy and paste the URL on the site you want to include the link.

4. Click the **OK** button to close the Link to This Post dialog box.

FIGURE 7.15   Select Link to This Post from the Options menu that opens.

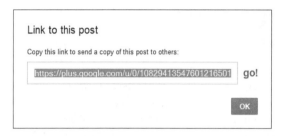

FIGURE 7.16   Copy the URL to link to it from your website or blog.

Reporting Abuse

If someone posts content that violates Google's terms and conditions, you can report it.

CAUTION: **Consider Carefully When to Report Content as Abuse**

You should report content only if it violates Google+ terms and conditions (spam, nudity, hate speech, violence, copyright, or child abuse). If someone simply posts content you don't like, you should just mute a specific post or remove this person from your circles rather than filing an abuse report.

To report abuse, follow these steps:

1. Click the down arrow in the upper-right corner of the post.

2. Select **Report Abuse** from the Options menu (refer to Figure 7.15).

3. In the Report This Post dialog box, shown in Figure 7.17, select the reason for reporting abuse: Spam, Nudity, Hate Speech or Violence, or Copyright.

4. Click the **Submit** button to submit your report to Google. Google reviews all reports of abuse and takes any necessary action.

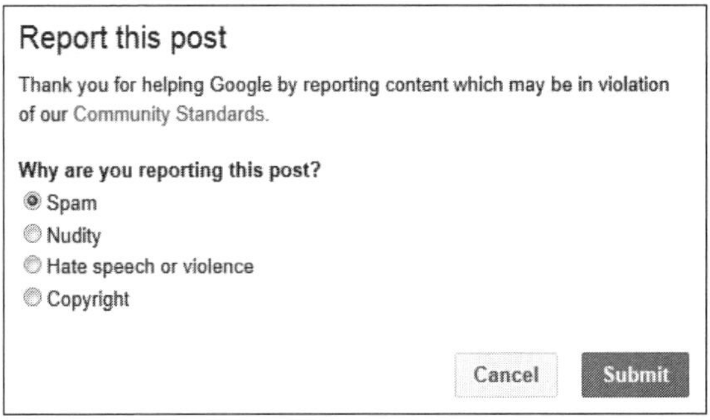

Report this post

Thank you for helping Google by reporting content which may be in violation of our Community Standards.

Why are you reporting this post?

◉ Spam
○ Nudity
○ Hate speech or violence
○ Copyright

Cancel   Submit

FIGURE 7.17   Let Google know why this post is abusive.

TIP: **Removing Someone from Your Circles If You Don't Like the Content This Person Posts**

If someone posts content you don't like but doesn't constitute abuse, consider simply removing this person from your circles. To do so, click the down arrow in the upper-right corner of the post and select Remove from Circles from the Options menu (refer to Figure 7.15).

Muting a Post

When you comment on a post, you receive a notification anytime someone else comments on that same post. Although you might want to read what your friends have to say about a pertinent topic, you might rather not receive a large volume of notifications about people you don't know. This is particularly common if you comment on a post that generates a lot of response from the Google+ community. To avoid this problem, you can mute the post. Muting removes a post from your stream and stops sending you notifications about future comments.

To mute a post, click the down arrow in the upper-right corner of the post and select **Mute This Post** from the Options menu (refer to Figure 7.15).

Google+ lets you know that the post is muted, as shown in Figure 7.18. To view the post again, click the **Undo Mute** link.

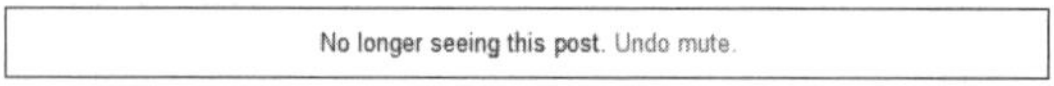

No longer seeing this post. Undo mute.

FIGURE 7.18   Mute posts that become overwhelmed with irrelevant chatter.

Viewing the Explore Page

To view the Google+ Explore page (see Figure 7.19), click the Explore icon on the Google+ ribbon.

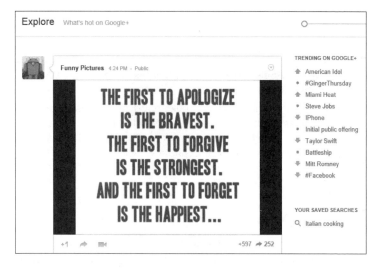

FIGURE 7.19   View interesting content from across Google+.

The Explore page displays the following:

▶ The What's Hot stream, which displays selected Google+ content that Google editors deem particularly interesting or relevant. To control how much What's Hot content displays in your main stream, use the slider in the upper-right corner of the page.

▶ Trending topics on Google+ (click a topic to view related posts)

▶ Links to any searches you've saved. See Lesson 8, "Searching on Google+," for more information about saved searches.

Summary

In this lesson, you learned how to manage your Google+ stream. Next, you'll learn how to search Google+ for specific people and content.

LESSON 8
Searching on Google+

In this lesson, you learn how to search Google+ for specific content.

Searching Google+ Content

If you're looking for a specific person, business, or brand, Google+ Search can help. You can also search for topics of interest to you, such as baking, camping, or the iPhone. The content that displays in Google+ search results includes the following:

▶ Google+ profiles and pages

▶ Google+ posts that other users shared directly with you

▶ Google+ public posts from people you may or may not know

▶ Trending content from external websites (such as content that a user recommended via the +1 button)

To search Google+, follow these steps:

1. Enter your search term in the search box at the top of Google+, shown in Figure 8.1.

FIGURE 8.1   Search for people, pages, and posts on Google+.

2. Google+ displays a list of the most likely matches in a drop-down menu. If you don't find a match in the list, click the **Search** button (a white magnifying glass on a blue rectangle).

3. Review the search results page for content that meets your search criteria. Figure 8.2 shows a sample search results page.

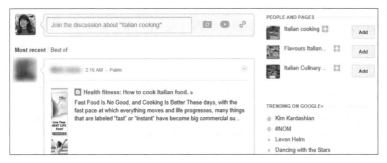

FIGURE 8.2   Explore Google+ content for your favorite interests.

On this page, you can

▶ View the top three matches for people and pages. To view more options, pause your mouse over the People and Pages section and click the **View All** link. You can add any of these people and pages to your Google+ circles by clicking their **Add** button.

▶ Join the conversation by posting your own related content. See Lesson 6, "Sharing Content on Google+," for more information about posting content in the share box.

▶ View content that matches your search term. This section includes posts shared directly on Google+ as well as web content that Google+ users recommended by using the +1 button. By default, Google+ displays the most recent content, but you can click the **Best Of** link to view the most popular, trending posts on a particular topic.

NOTE: **Google+ Posts Display in Real-Time**

When you use the default option (Most Recent) for displaying posts on a Google+ results page, new posts arrive in real-time on your page. To pause real-time results, click the **Pause** button. Note that this button displays only after real-time content is available for your search term. This feature is more likely to become active if you searched for a popular topic.

Filtering Google+ Search Results

If Google+ displays too many options, you can filter your search results. By default, Google+ displays everything related to your search topic (see Figure 8.2). However, you can narrow your search results by clicking the **Everything** button and selecting one of the following options from the menu: People and pages, Google+ posts, Sparks, Hangouts, From your circles, From you, or From this location.

Saving a Google+ Search

If you're interested in a particular search topic, saving it gives you easy access to new content in the future.

To save a search, click the **Save This Search** button on the search results page (refer to Figure 8.2).

Google+ displays a link for this topic in the Your Saved Searches section of the Explore page. For example, saving the results for your "Italian cooking" search displays an Italian Cooking link, as shown in Figure 8.3. See Lesson 7, "Viewing Your Google+ Stream," for more information about the Explore page.

Whenever you want to view new Google+ content related to this search term, you can click this link.

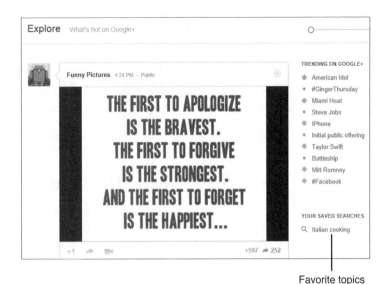

Favorite topics

FIGURE 8.3   Links to your favorite topics are available on the Explore page.

Summary

In this lesson, you learned how to search Google+ by keyword, filter search results, and save your searches. Next, you learn how to view and manage your Google+ notifications.

LESSON 9

Viewing and Managing Notifications

In this lesson, you learn how to view and manage notifications.

Understanding Google+ Notifications

Notifications alert you to important activities on Google+. You receive a notification whenever someone

- ▶ Adds you to one of their Google+ circles

- ▶ Tags you in a photo

- ▶ Shares a post with you directly

- ▶ Adds a comment to one of your posts

- ▶ Endorses one of your posts using the +1 button

- ▶ Mentions you in a post

- ▶ Invites you to a game or sends you a game gift

You can view your notifications on Google+, receive notifications via email, or receive notifications via text message (SMS).

Viewing Your Notifications on Google+

The Notifications button in the upper-right corner of Google+ tells you how many unread notifications you have by highlighting this number in red. Figure 9.1, for example, shows three unread notifications.

FIGURE 9.1   Your number of unread notifications is highlighted in red.

> NOTE: **Why Isn't the Notifications Button Red?**
> If you don't have any unread notifications, the button displays the number zero (0) and isn't highlighted in red. You can still click the Notifications button to view previously read notifications.

To view and react to your notifications, follow these steps:

1. Click the **Notifications** button in the upper-right corner of any Google+ page (refer to Figure 9.1). Figure 9.2 shows some sample notifications. Google+ groups your notifications by type, such as notifications that let you know someone added you to a circle.

FIGURE 9.2   View your notifications by type.

2. Click the arrow to the right of a notification to view its detail menu, as shown in Figure 9.3. For example, you can view all the people who recently added you to a circle.

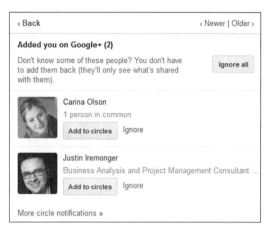

FIGURE 9.3   View the people associated with each notification type.

3. Take any of the following actions:

▶ Click someone's name to open that person's profile.

▶ Pause your mouse over someone's name to view a pop-up box that includes this person's headline, as shown in Figure 9.4.

▶ Pause your mouse over the **Add to Circles** button below the name of a person you want to add to a circle. In the pop-up box that opens (see Figure 9.5), select the check box next to the circle to which you want to add this person. Optionally, click the **Create New Circle** link to add this person to a new circle. If you've already added someone to a circle, the Add to Circles button is replaced with a button that displays the name of the circle this person belongs to.

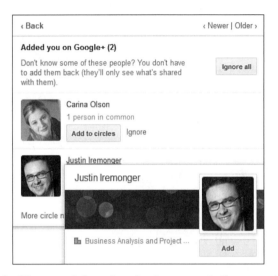

FIGURE 9.4   View more information about someone in the pop-up box.

FIGURE 9.5   Quickly add people to circles.

▶ Click the **Ignore** link to ignore someone who appears on the Notifications menu. For example, you can ignore someone you don't know and don't plan to add to one of your circles. If you change your mind, click **Undo**. After clicking the Ignore link, Google+ enables you to click the **Block** link, which blocks someone from Google+. Blocking is a stronger action than hiding. When you block people on Google+, they will no longer be in any of your

circles and they can't comment on your posts. The people
you block are not aware that you have blocked them. See
Lesson 7, "Viewing Your Google+ Stream," for more information about the ramifications of blocking people.

From the Notifications detail menu, you can also do the following:

▶ Click the **Back** link to return to the initial Notifications menu.

▶ Click the **Older** link or **Newer** link to move to older or newer
notifications.

▶ Click the **More Circle Notifications** link to open the
Notifications page, where you can view all your notifications in
one place. Clicking the **View All Notifications** link on the initial
Notifications menu also opens this page. See "Viewing the
Notifications Page" for more information about this page.

To close the Notifications menu, click another part of the Google+ screen.

Viewing the Notifications Page

The Notifications page enables you to view all your notifications in one
place. To access this page, click the **View All Notifications** link on the
Notifications menu (refer to Figure 9.2). Figure 9.6 shows the
Notifications page.

On this page, you can:

▶ Interact with a notification by clicking one of the available links
or buttons. The actions available depend on the type of notification and your connection with the people involved. For example,
when someone who isn't in one of your circles adds you,
Google+ displays the Add to Circles button for this person.
When someone tags you in a photo album, Google+ displays
links to that person's profile and the album.

▶ View notifications about people adding you to circles by clicking
the **Circle Adds** button.

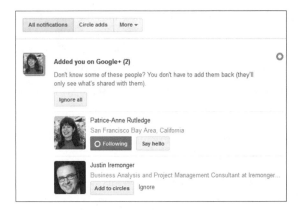

FIGURE 9.6   View all your notifications on one page.

▶ Filter your notifications by clicking the **More** button at the top and selecting one of the following options from the drop-down menu: Your Posts, Mentions of You, Photos of You, Other Peoples' Posts, and Games.

▶ Click the down arrow to the right of any notification to hide the notification or report abuse. Note that you can't hide or report notifications about people who add you to circles, but you can choose to ignore or block individual people.

▶ Click the down arrow to the right of a game notification and select **Mute All Game Notifications** from the menu if you don't want Google+ to notify you about your gaming activities.

Receiving Notifications via Email and Text Message

If you prefer, you can receive notifications by email or text message (SMS). Google+ enables you to filter the notifications you receive if you don't want to receive every notification in this manner. For example, you could receive a notification by email whenever someone adds you to a circle or mentions your name, receive a notification by text message whenever someone starts a Messenger conversation with you, and read all other notifications directly on Google+.

To specify your notification delivery preferences, click the **Home** icon on the Google+ ribbon and select **Settings** from the drop-down menu in the upper-right corner of the page. For more information, see Lesson 5, "Managing Google+ Settings and Privacy."

Specifying Who Can Send You Notifications

Google+ enables you to specify the people who can send you notifications. This is most useful for users with many people in circles who are very active on Google+. Using this feature you can control notifications when someone mentions you, shares content directly with you, tags you, or invites you to a hangout. For example, you can restrict this activity only to people in your circles, your extended circles, or a custom selection of circles.

To specify who can send you notifications, click the **Home** icon on the Google+ ribbon and select **Settings** from the drop-down menu in the upper-right corner of the page. For more information, see Lesson 5.

Summary

In this lesson, you learned how to view and manage Google+ notifications. Now it's time to learn more about the many photo options Google+ provides.

LESSON 10

Working with Photos

In this lesson, you learn how to upload, edit, and manage photos.

Exploring Google+ Photo Options

Google+ offers a comprehensive photo management solution, enabling you to upload, store, and share unlimited photos. You can upload photos up to 2,048 x 2,048 pixels in size. Google+ resizes photos larger than this.

Your photos display on the stream as well as on the Photos tab of your profile. Optionally, you can hide this tab. You also maintain complete control over who can view your photos. For example, you can share photos on the stream publicly, or share only with people in specific circles or your extended circle.

> NOTE: **Google+ Integrates with Picasa Web Albums**
>
> Google+ integrates directly with Picasa Web Albums (http://picasaweb.google.com), Google's digital photo-management web application. When you upload photos to Google+, they are automatically available on Picasa Web Albums as well (all Google+ users receive an account for this app). As with Google+, you have complete control over who can view your web albums.

Uploading Photos to Google+

Google+ provides several places to upload and share photos:

 ▶ **From the share box.** You can access this box on your stream or by clicking the **Share** button in the upper-right corner of the page. Click the **Add Photos** icon in the lower-right corner of the share box to upload photos from your computer, create a photo album, or upload photos from your iPhone or Android smart-phone. See Lesson 6, "Sharing Content on Google+," for more information.

▶ **From the Google+ ribbon.** Pause your mouse over the Photos icon on the ribbon and click the **Add Photos** button on the pop-out menu.

▶ **From the Google+ Photos page.** Click the **Upload New Photos** button to create a photo album. See "Creating and Managing Photo Albums" later in this lesson for more information.

▶ **From the Photos tab on your profile.** Click the **Upload New Photos** button to create a photo album. See "Creating and Manag-ing Photo Albums" later in this lesson for more information.

Exploring the Photos Page

The Photos page offers a centralized location to manage your photos and photo albums on Google+. To access the Photos page, click the **Photos** icon on the Google+ ribbon. Figure 10.1 shows the Photos page with the default tab selected, From Phone.

FIGURE 10.1   View, upload, and manage your photos on the Photos page.

The Photos page has four tabs:

▶ **From Phone.** View and manage photos you uploaded from your phone. You must have an iPhone or Android smartphone and download the Google+ app to use this feature. Google+ uploads the photos you take from your phone and places them on this tab, where they remain private until you choose to share them. Click the appropriate **Google+ App** button to download from either Google Play or the iPhone App Store.

▶ **Albums.** Add, view, and manage photo albums. See "Creating and Managing Photo Albums" for more information.

▶ **From Posts.** View photos you added to your Google+ posts.

▶ **Photos of You.** View photos tagged with your name. Note that even if you upload a profile photo of yourself, you need to tag it with your name for it to display on this tab. See "Tagging Photos" later in this lesson for more information.

Creating and Managing Photo Albums

A photo album is a collection of photos, usually on a specific topic or taken at a specific place or event. You can post and share photo albums on Google+ just like you do individual photos.

TIP: **Use a Photo Album to Post a Slide Deck on Google+**
You can also use a photo album to post a slide deck on Google+. For example, export all the slides in a PowerPoint presentation to images and post them as an album. Your Google+ network can comment on each slide/photo individually or on the presentation as a whole.

Google+ enables you to create a photo album from the share box on your stream and on the upper-right corner of any Google+ page, the Photos page, or the Photos tab on your profile. The process is similar for all three.

Creating a Photo Album

To create a photo album from the Photos page, follow these steps:

1. Click the **Photos** icon on the Google+ ribbon.

2. Click the **Upload New Photos** button in the upper-right corner of the page.

3. In the Upload and Share Photos dialog box, enter a name for your photo album in the **Album Name** field. By default, Google+ displays the current date as your album name, but changing this to a more meaningful name makes it easier to identify your photo albums.

4. Click the **Select Photos from Your Computer** button.

5. In the File Upload dialog box, select the photos you want to add and click the **Open** button. Depending on your operating system and browser, this dialog box and button might have different names.

6. Your selected photos display in the Upload and Share Photos dialog box, shown in Figure 10.2. Optionally, click the photo to add a caption, rotate it left or right, or delete it. You can also edit photos using the lightbox. See "Working in the Photo Lightbox" later in this lesson for more information.

FIGURE 10.2   View, rotate, or delete the photos you upload.

7. Optionally, click the **Upload More** link if you want to upload additional photos for this album. You can also add more photos after you create your album.

8. Click the **Create Album** button in the lower-right corner of the dialog box.

9. In the Share Album dialog box, you can choose the people and circles you want to share your album with. You can share your album now or at a later time. Sharing an album displays it on the Google+ stream of everyone you share with. See "Sharing an Album" later in this lesson for more information. If you don't want to share this album right now, click the **Cancel** button.

Your new album now displays on the Albums tab on the Photos page. See the "Viewing Your Photo Albums" section for more information about this tab.

Viewing Your Photo Albums

To view your photo albums, pause your mouse over the Photos icon on the Google+ ribbon and select **Albums** from the pop-out menu. You can also access your albums by clicking the **Albums** tab on the Photos page. On the Albums tab, you can do the following:

▶ View a collection of photos from your posts, your profile photos, your scrapbook photos, and your photo albums. Figure 10.3 shows a sample of the Albums tab.

FIGURE 10.3   View all your photo albums in one place.

▶ Determine who you're sharing the album with by looking at the small icon next to each album. Pause your mouse over the icon to view its description. For example, a red circle with a diagonal line means that only you can view this album.

▶ Click an album to open its detail page, where you can view the photos it contains as well as rename, share, or delete it. In the album, click an individual photo to open it in lightbox view, where you can edit it.

▶ Click the **Sharing Settings** link to specify sharing options for each of your albums.

Sharing an Album

You can share a photo album when you create it or at any time after that.

To share a photo album, follow these steps:

1. Pause your mouse over the Photos icon on the Google+ ribbon and select **Albums** from the pop-out menu. You can also access your albums by clicking the **Albums** tab on the Photos page.

2. Select the album you want to share.

3. Click the **Share** button on the album detail page, as shown in Figure 10.4.

FIGURE 10.4   Share your photo album with others on Google+.

4. In the Share Album dialog box (see Figure 10.5), enter any introductory text about your album in the text box. For example, you could explain where you took these photos, why you're posting them, or what feedback you want from the people you're sharing with.

Share album "Hong Kong Vacation Photos"

Add a comment...

O Family ×   + Add more people

Share   Cancel

FIGURE 10.5   Choose exactly who you want to share with.

5. Specify who you want to share this album with. By default, Google+ displays your most recent sharing choices. For example, if you last shared a post with your Friends circle, that's what displays here. You can share with this same group of people or click the **Add More People** link to select other people to share with. For example, you can share with the people in one or more circles, your extended circles (friends of friends), the general public, or one specific person (enter this person's name in the text box). For a reminder on how to share on Google+, see Lesson 6.

6. Optionally, click the down arrow in the lower-right corner to select either **Disable Comments** or **Lock This Post** from the menu. Disabling comments prevents other users from commenting on your photo album post. Locking your post prevents people from sharing it.

7. Click the **Share** button to post your album on the stream, where only the people you shared with can view it. Figure 10.6 shows a sample shared album.

FIGURE 10.6   Display your album on the Google+ stream.

TIP: **Share Your Photo Album via a Link**

If you would like to share your photo album with a link, select Share Album via Link from the **More** drop-down menu. This opens a dialog box that displays a Web URL that you can share with others.

Updating Album Sharing Settings

If you change your mind about how your photo albums are shared, you can update these settings.

To update your sharing settings, follow these steps:

1. Pause your mouse over the Photos icon on the Google+ ribbon and select **Albums** from the pop-out menu.

2. Click the **Share Settings** button to open the Change How Your Albums Are Shared dialog box, shown in Figure 10.7.

3. From the drop-down list next to each album, select your sharing preference. Options include: Public, Extended Circles, Your Circles, Limited (you can choose who to share with), and Only You (private).

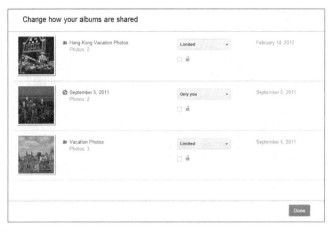

FIGURE 10.7   At any time you can change how your albums are shared.

4. If you want to disable resharing, tagging, and + mentioning, select the check box next to the Lock icon.

5. Click the **Done** button to save your changes and close the dialog box.

Organizing an Album

Google+ makes it easy to rearrange the photos in your albums. This is particularly useful for a scrapbook album you display on your profile.

To organize a photo album, follow these steps:

1. Pause your mouse over the Photos icon on the Google+ ribbon and select **Albums** from the pop-out menu.

2. Select the album you want to organize.

3. Select **Organize Album** from the More drop-down menu to open the Organize Album page (see Figure 10.8).

FIGURE 10.8   Quickly organize your Google+ photo albums.

4. On this page, you can:

    ▶ Select and drag photos to organize them.

    ▶ Select one or more photos and click the **Move** button to move your selection to another album. You can also create a new album for your selected photos.

    ▶ Select one or more photos and click the **Delete** button to delete your selection.

    ▶ Select a photo and click the **Move to Top** button or **Move to Bottom** button to rearrange the order in which the photo displays.

    ▶ Click the **Order by Date** button to arrange your photos by date.

5. Click the **Done Organizing** button to save your changes and close the dialog box.

Deleting an Album

If you no longer want to keep a photo album, or if you made a mistake and want to start over, you can delete it.

To delete a photo album, follow these steps:

1. Pause your mouse over the Photos icon on the Google+ ribbon and select **Albums** from the pop-out menu.

2. Select the album you want to delete.

3. Select **Delete Album** from the More drop-down menu.

4. Click the **Delete** button in the dialog box that opens to confirm that you want to delete this album. Google+ permanently deletes the album.

Adding Photos to an Existing Album

You can add photos to any existing photo album, following a process similar to creating your initial album.

To add more photos to an existing album, follow these steps:

1. Pause your mouse over the Photos icon on the Google+ ribbon and select **Albums** from the pop-out menu.

2. Select the album to which you want to add more photos.

3. Click the **Add Photos** button on the album detail page (refer to Figure 10.4).

4. Click the **Select Photos from Your Computer** button.

5. In the File Upload dialog box, select the photos you want to add and click the **Open** button. Depending on your operating system and browser, this dialog box and button might have different names.

6. The Add Photos dialog box displays your photos. Optionally, click a photo to add a caption, rotate it left or right, or delete it. You can also edit photos using the lightbox.

7. Click the **Add Photos** button in the lower-right corner of the dialog box.

8. In the Share Album dialog box, you can choose the people and circles you want to share your updated album with. You can share your album now or share it at a later time. See "Sharing an Album" earlier in this lesson for more information. If you don't want to share this album right now, click the **Cancel** button.

Your updated album appears on the Albums tab on the Photos page. You might have to open your album again to view the new photos.

Working in the Photo Lightbox

The Google+ photo lightbox enables you to view, tag, caption, comment on, edit, delete, and manage your photos. Click a photo to open it in light-box view, shown in Figure 10.9.

FIGURE 10.9   Lightbox view enables you to manage and edit photos.

You can click a photo in your stream, on any of the tabs on the Photos page, or on your profile's Photos tab. The editing features available depend on whether you uploaded the photo or someone else did.

TIP: **Turn on Find My Face to Help People Tag You in Photos**
The first time you open a photo in the lightbox, the Help People Tag You in Photos dialog box opens. Click the **Turn on Find My Face** button if you want Google+ to prompt the people in your circles to tag you in photos. Otherwise, click the **No Thanks** button to close the dialog box.

Exploring the Lightbox

In lightbox view, you can do the following:

- ▶ **Scroll through album photos.** Click the large arrows to the left and right of a photo to scroll through an album with a large number of photos.

- ▶ **Rotate a photo to the left.** Click the **Rotate Left** button in the upper-left corner of the page to rotate the photo 180 degrees to the left.

- ▶ **Rotate a photo to the right.** Click the **Rotate Right** button in the upper-left corner of the page to rotate the photo 180 degrees to the right.

- ▶ **Turn on Autofix.** Click the **Autofix** button in the upper-left corner of the page to adjust photo flaws automatically.

- ▶ **Edit a photo in Creative Kit.** Click the **Edit Photo** button in the upper-left corner of the page. See "Editing Photos Using Creative Kit" later in this lesson for more information.

- ▶ **Add a caption.** Pause your mouse over the existing caption, which displays below your profile photo in the upper-right corner of the page. If you didn't add a caption when you uploaded a photo, this field displays as "Add Caption." Click the **Edit** link, enter your caption, and click the Save Caption button.

- ▶ **Add a tag.** Click the **Tag People** link in the sidebar to add a tag to a photo. See "Tagging Photos" later in this lesson for more information.

▶ **Add a comment.** Add your own commentary about the photo in the **Add a Comment** box in the lightbox sidebar. Click the **Post Comment** button to post your comment.

▶ **Download a full-size photo.** Select **Download Full Size** from the Options drop-down list to download and save a full-size version of this photo.

▶ **View photo details.** Select **Photo Details** from the Options drop-down list to view details about this photo, such as its dimensions, file size, exposure, aperture, and more.

▶ **Report or delete comments.** Select **Manage Comments** from the Options drop-down list. Be aware that this menu option is available only if your photo has comments. On the right side of the page (see Figure 10.10), click the **Delete Comment** button below a comment to delete it or the **Flag as Inappropriate** button below a comment to report it to Google+.

FIGURE 10.10   Delete or report any inappropriate photo comments.

▶ **Delete a photo.** Select **Delete Photo** from the Options drop-down list to delete the photo. Click **OK** in the dialog box that opens to confirm permanent deletion.

NOTE: **You Can't Edit a Photo You Didn't Upload**
If you're viewing a photo in lightbox view that someone else uploaded, you can add a comment, add a tag, view photo details, and report abuse, but you can't edit or delete the photo.

Tagging Photos

Tagging photos offers a way to identify the people in them. Google+ also gives you complete control over how and when others can tag you.

Tagging a Photo

To tag yourself or someone else in a photo, follow these steps:

1. Click a photo to open it in lightbox view.

2. Click the **double-arrow** button on the photo, shown in Figure 10.11.

FIGURE 10.11   Tag photos in lightbox view.

> NOTE: **Google+ Recognizes Photos with Multiple People**
>
> If your photo includes multiple people, Google+ displays a box around each person's face when you pause your mouse over the photo. Click the **Click Face to Tag** text box below each person to tag that person. Automatic recognition doesn't work for all photos, but you can also tag a photo manually by clicking the **Add a New Tag** button in the sidebar.

3. Click the **Tag** button on the right side of the photo to display a circle around the person's face.

4. In the text box, start typing the name of the person you want to tag, select the appropriate person from the drop-down list of Google+ users, and press **Enter** to save your tag. Figure 10.12 shows an example of adding a tag.

5. Click the **Close** (x) button in the upper-right corner of the screen to close the photo in lightbox view.

If you tag a photo of yourself, it displays on the Photos of You tab on the Photos page.

If you tag a photo of someone else, that person is notified of your tag and has the option to approve or remove the tag.

FIGURE 10.12   Select the name of a Google+ user to tag this photo.

Approving or Removing a Tag

When someone tags you in a photo, Google+ sends you a notification about this tag, allowing you to approve or remove it. By default, Google+ automatically approves tags from people in your circles. You can change this option, however. See "Specifying Photo Tag Approval Settings" later in this lesson for more information.

To respond to a photo tag notification, follow these steps.

1. Click the **Notifications** button in the upper-right corner of any Google+ page.

2. Scroll down to the photo notification you want to review or click the **View All Notifications** link to view additional notifications on the Notifications page.

> TIP: **Filter to Display Only All Photo Tag Notifications**
> To display only your photo tag notifications, select **Photos of You** from the More drop-down list in the upper-right corner of the Notifications page.

3. Google+ displays the current status of the tag below the photo. For example, in Figure 10.13, the tag is already approved because someone in one of your circles added it. If you want to accept the photo tag, you don't need to do anything. If you want to remove the photo tag, click the **Remove** (x) button.

Google+ displays photos tagged with your name on the Photos of You tab on the Photos page.

FIGURE 10.13   You can accept or remove photo tags.

Removing a Photo Tag in Lightbox View

You can also remove photo tags in lightbox view.

To do so, follow these steps:

   1. Click a photo to open it in lightbox view.

   2. Pause your mouse over the tag you want to remove on the page's right sidebar and click the **Remove This Tag** (small x) button (see Figure 10.14).

FIGURE 10.14   Remove photo tags in lightbox view.

   3. Click the **OK** button in the dialog box that opens to confirm deletion.

Specifying Photo Tag Approval Settings

By default, Google+ automatically approves photo tags from anyone in your circles. You can change this default setting, however.

To specify whose tags you want Google+ to automatically approve, follow these steps:

1. Click the **Home** icon on the Google+ ribbon and select **Settings** from the drop-down menu in the upper-right corner of the page.

2. Scroll down the Google+ tab to locate the Photos section at the bottom of the page, as shown in Figure 10.15.

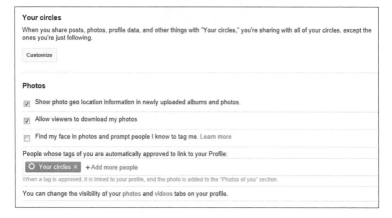

FIGURE 10.15   You're in control of the photo tags Google+ automatically approves.

3. Click the **Remove** icon (x) to the right of the Your Circles chip to require your manual approval for a photo tag. Google+ sends you a notification about any tag requiring approval and also displays pending tag approvals on the Photos of You tab on the Photos page.

TIP: **Automatically Approve the Photo Tags Only of People in Specific Circles**

If you want to give only certain circles automatic approval, click the **Add More People** link and select the appropriate circles. For example, you might want to automatically approve everyone in the Family and Friends circles, but not the Acquaintances or Following circles.

Google+ requires your approval anytime someone tags you whose tags aren't preapproved. See "Approving or Removing a Tag" earlier in this lesson for more information.

You can also specify photo tag approval settings when you edit the Photos tab on your profile.

Editing Photos Using Creative Kit

Google+ enables you to apply special effects and improve the quality of photos you upload using Creative Kit.

To edit a photo in Creative Kit, follow these steps:

1. Select a photo to open it in lightbox view.

2. Click the **Edit Photo** button in the upper-left corner of the page.

3. Edit your photo using Creative Kit (see Figure 10.16). Using this tool, you can crop, rotate, adjust exposure, modify colors, sharpen, resize, add special effects, add text, and more.

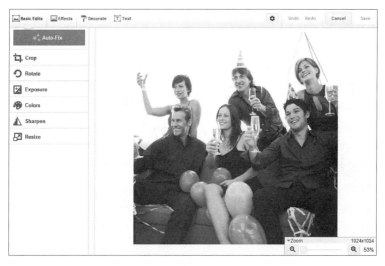

FIGURE 10.16   Apply effects to your photos.

4. If you don't like an effect, click the **Undo** button and try a different effect.

5. If you're satisfied with the effect you applied, click the **Save** button.

Summary

In this lesson, you learned how to upload, manage, and edit photos in Google+. Next, get chatting with Google+ Chat.

LESSON 11

Chatting on Google+

In this lesson, you learn how to chat on Google+, using text, voice, and video.

Understanding Google+ Chat

Google+ enables you to communicate directly with other users through its chat functionality. You can chat in a text-based chat window, optionally enhanced with voice or video chat.

Exploring the Chat List

The chat list displays on the right side of most Google+ pages, as shown in Figure 11.1.

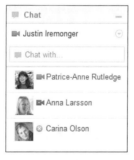

FIGURE 11.1   Color-coded icons let you know who is available to chat.

If the chat list doesn't display on the right side of the page, it's been minimized to the lower-right corner of Google+ (see Figure 11.2). Click the right side of the minimized window to restore the chat list.

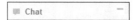

FIGURE 11.2   Maximize the chat list to start chatting.

Google+ uses color-coded icons to communicate the availability of the people in your chat list:

▶ **Green.** Online and available to chat.

▶ **Yellow.** Idle. Google+ automatically switches a person's status to idle after 15 minutes of inactivity.

▶ **Red.** Busy (online, but unavailable to chat). Google+ users can display this status if they don't want to chat with others. For example, people who are at work might not be available to chat with friends.

▶ **Gray.** Offline or signed out of chat. Google+ users can display this status by selecting the Invisible status, even if they are still online.

See "Specifying Your Chat Availability" for more information about how to manually change your own status.

If users haven't enabled voice and video chat, availability is designated by a color-coded circle. If they have enabled voice and video chat (either in Google+ or another Google product), the circle becomes a color-coded video icon.

See "Using Voice and Video Chat" later in this lesson for more information about enabling this feature.

Specifying Your Chat Availability

By default, you're listed as available in the chat list (refer to Figure 11.1).

To change your availability status, click the down arrow to the right of your name in this chat list and select one of the following options from the drop-down menu (see Figure 11.3):

- ▶ Available (the default)

- ▶ Busy

- ▶ Invisible (changes your status to Offline)

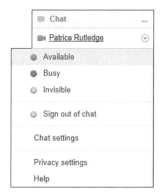

FIGURE 11.3   You're in control of the chat availability you display to other Google+ users.

Specifying Your Chat Privacy Settings

By default, Google+ enables you to chat with people in your circles who also have you in their circles.

To restrict chat to specific circles, follow these steps:

1. Click the down arrow to the right of your name in the chat list and select **Privacy Settings** from the drop-down menu (refer to Figure 11.3).

2. In the pop-up box, click the **Your Circles** button and select **Custom** from the drop-down menu. The box expands with a list of your available circles, as shown in Figure 11.4.

3. Select the check box to the left of every circle you want to enable for chat.

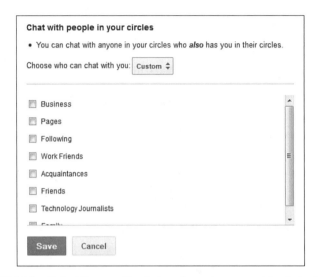

FIGURE 11.4   Select the specific circles of people you want to chat with.

4. Click the **Save** button to save your changes. People in circles for which you've disabled chat no longer display in your chat list. You can no longer initiate a chat with them, and they can no longer initiate a chat with you.

Chatting on Google+

Google+ offers several options for chatting. You can participate in a text-based chat or enhance your conversation with voice and video chat.

Participating in a Chat

To chat with someone, follow these steps:

1. Click the name of the person you want to chat with in the chat list that displays on the right side of the page (refer to Figure 11.1). A green icon displays before the names of people available to chat. See "Exploring the Chat List" earlier in this lesson for more information about the other icons in this list.

2. If you want to chat with someone who doesn't display on your chat list, start typing that person's name in the text box below your name and select from the drop-down list of users (see Figure 11.5). Be aware that you might not be able to find everyone in your Google+ circles. For example, you won't see people who haven't enabled chat or who have disabled chat for your circle.

FIGURE 11.5   Search for people to chat with.

3. The chat window opens in the lower-right corner of the screen (see Figure 11.6). Type your chat message in the text box and press the Enter key. Your message displays in the chat window of your recipient, who can then respond to you (see Figure 11.7). If a recipient is offline, the chat window lets you know this.

FIGURE 11.6   Conduct chats in the chat window, which displays in the lower-right corner of your screen.

4. Continue conducting your chat in the chat window.

5. When you're finished chatting, click the **Close (x)** icon in the upper-right corner of the chat window.

FIGURE 11.7   Your message as your recipient sees it.

During your chat, you can do the following:

▶ Minimize the chat window when you're not actively chatting by clicking the **Minimize** icon in the upper-right corner of the chat window.

▶ Open a separate window for chatting by clicking the **Pop-out** icon in the upper-right corner of the chat window.

▶ Use emoticons in your chat, such as a smiley face, sad face, or heart. To do so, click the smiley face icon in the lower-right corner on the chat window. A pop-up box with numerous emoticon possibilities opens, as shown in Figure 11.8. You can select any of these to add a personal touch to your chats. Google+ converts any text-based emoticon you enter—such as ":-)" to create a smiley face—to a graphic icon in your chat.

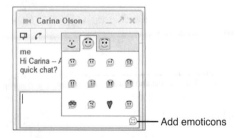

FIGURE 11.8   Add some emotion to text chats with emoticons.

Sending a File

If you're discussing a file with someone on Google+, you can send the file to this person via the chat window. For example, you can send Word documents, presentations, spreadsheets, or photos to another Google+ user.

To a send a file from the chat window, follow these steps:

1. In the chat window, select **Send a File** from the More drop-down list (see Figure 11.9).

FIGURE 11.9   Send files to the people you chat with.

2. In the File Upload dialog box, select the file you want to send and click the **Open** button. Depending on your operating system and browser, the names of this dialog box and button could vary. The Chat window notifies you that you're sharing a file, as shown in Figure 11.10.

FIGURE 11.10   The chat window lets you know your file was sent.

3. Google+ alerts the recipient of the file, prompting this person to click the **Accept** link to open or save it.

4. When the recipient accepts your file, the chat window alerts you that the transfer is completed.

Using Voice and Video Chat

You can add free, computer-to-computer voice and video chat to your Google+ chats using a simple plug-in. This plug-in requires one of the following operating systems:

▶ Windows XP Service Pack 3 or later

▶ Intel Mac OS X 10.5 or later

▶ Linux

In addition, you also need a microphone, speakers, and webcam to use voice and video chat.

If you use chat using another Google product such as Gmail or iGoogle, you might already have this plug-in installed. If not, you can set it up from the Google+ chat window.

NOTE: **Check Out Google+ Hangouts for Video Chat**

If you want to participate in video chats, also check out Google+ Hangouts, which enables you to chat with multiple people. You can start a hangout from the chat window by clicking the **Start a Hangout** icon in the upper-left corner. See Lesson 12, "Using Hangouts for Video Chat," for more information.

Setting Up Voice and Video Chat

To add voice and video chat, follow these steps:

1. In the chat window, click the **Start Voice Chat** icon (see Figure 11.11).

2. Click the **Click Here** link to add voice and video chat.

Start voice chat

FIGURE 11.11 Setting up voice and video chat gives you more chat options.

3. The Chat Face to Face with Family and Friends page opens in a new window (see Figure 11.12). You can also navigate to this page directly at www.google.com/chat/video. Click the **Install Voice and Video Chat** button to install this plug-in. You might have to click the **Allow** button to continue installation.

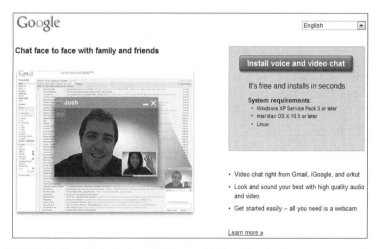

FIGURE 11.12 Click the Install Voice and Video Chat button to get started.

4. After installation is complete, close your browser and sign back in again.

5. On the chat list, click the down arrow to the right of your name
and select **Chat Settings** from the menu.

6. In the Chat Settings dialog box, shown in Figure 11.13, click the
Verify Your Settings link to verify that your camera, microphone, and speakers work properly. Optionally, you can select the
appropriate camera, microphone, and speakers from the drop-
down lists.

FIGURE 11.13   Verify your settings before starting to chat.

7. By default, Google+

- ▶ Enables echo cancellation, which helps reduce echo sounds
  during voice chats.

- ▶ Disables high-resolution video.

- ▶ Reports quality statistics to help improve voice and video
  chat.

- ▶ Plays a sound notification when new chat messages arrive
  (this feature requires Flash).

You can retain these default settings or change them by selecting or deselecting the related check box.

8. Click the **Save Changes** button to save your changes and close the dialog box.

You're now ready to use voice and video chat. Google+ displays the video icon next to your status on the chat list (refer to Figure 11.1).

Participating in a Voice Chat

To add voice chat to an existing chat, follow these steps:

1. In the chat window, click the **Start Voice Chat** icon (see Figure 11.14).

FIGURE 11.14 You can start a voice chat from the chat window.

2. Google+ alerts the person you're chatting with that you would like to start a voice chat, as shown in Figure 11.15. This person must have enabled the voice and video plug-in and click the **Answer** button to participate in the call. If someone hasn't enabled this plug-in yet, you can send an invite by selecting **Invite [First Name] to Voice/Video Chat** from the More drop-down list.

3. Conduct your voice chat.

4. When you're done talking, click the **End** button to end the voice chat.

5. Click the **Close (x)** icon in the upper-right corner of the chat window to close it.

FIGURE 11.15   The person you want to talk with must answer your voice chat request.

Participating in a Video Chat

To add video chat to an existing chat, follow these steps:

1. In the chat window, select **Start Video Chat** from the More drop-down list (refer to Figure 11.9).

2. Google+ alerts the person you're chatting with that you would like to start a video chat. This person must have enabled the voice and video plug-in, have a webcam, and click the **Answer** button to participate in the video chat.

3. Conduct your video chat, as shown in Figure 11.16.

4. When you're done, click the **End** button to end the video chat.

5. Click the **Close (x)** icon in the upper-right corner of the chat window to close it.

Chatting Off the Record

By default, Google+ retains a record of your chats in Gmail. You must have a Gmail account to use this feature. To view a record of your Google+ chats with a Gmail contact, pause your mouse over this person's name in the Gmail chat list and select **Recent Conversations** from the Video & More drop-down menu (see Figure 11.17). If you haven't enabled video, this menu is called the More menu.

If you don't want to save a record of your chats with someone, however, you can go off the record with that person. Google+ notifies the person you're chatting with when you choose to go off or on the record.

FIGURE 11.16   Participating in a video chat.

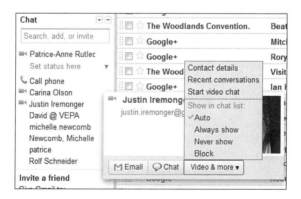

FIGURE 11.17   Google+ retains a record of your chats in Gmail.

When chatting with someone in the chat window, select **Go Off the Record** from the More drop-down list (refer to Figure 11.9).

If you want to go back on the record again with this person, click the **Cancel** link.

Signing Out of Chat

You can sign out of chat completely and hide your availability from your contacts. (You'll display as Offline.) To do so, click the down arrow to the right of your name in the chat list and select **Sign Out of Chat** from the drop-down menu (see Figure 11.18).

FIGURE 11.18   Sign out of chat when you don't want to display in the chat list of your Google+ friends.

You won't be able to chat again until you sign back into chat by clicking the **Sign Into Chat** link below the chat list. If you want to maintain a chat conversation with someone, but not be available to others, you should change your status to Invisible rather than sign out of Chat entirely.

TIP: **Getting More Help with Google+ Chat**
Although Google+ Chat is easy to use after you set it up, technical issues could complicate matters. If you follow the instructions in this lesson and still have problems with Chat, click the down arrow to the right of your name in the chat list and select **Help** from the drop-down menu.

Summary

In this lesson, you learned how to chat on Google+. Next, it's time to get visual with Google+ Hangouts for video chat.

Using Hangouts for Video Chat

In this lesson, you learn how to use Google+ Hangouts to conduct a video chat.

Understanding Hangouts

Although Google+ offers many ways to share, connect, and collaborate with others, there are times when you can't beat face-to-face communication. For those times, Google+ offers Hangouts.

PLAIN ENGLISH: **Hangouts**

Google+ Hangouts enable you to participate in live video chats with up to 10 other Google+ users. Using Hangouts, you can casually chat with people in your circles or plan a hangout with specific people. You can also incorporate YouTube videos into your hangouts.

Preparing to Use Hangouts

Before getting started with Hangouts, be sure that you have all the required equipment, software, and plug-ins.

To participate in a hangout, you must

▶ Use a computer with a 2Ghz dual-core processor or greater and one of the following operating systems: Windows 7, Windows Vista with SP1 or later, Windows XP, Mac OS X 10.5+, Chrome, or Linux.

▶ Have a webcam, microphone, and speakers. A headset is optional
    but produces better audio results.

▶ Use one of the following browsers: Google Chrome 10+,
    Microsoft Internet Explorer 8+, Mozilla Firefox 3+, or Safari 4+.

▶ Have bandwidth of 900kbps (up/down) for one-on-one hangouts
    or 900kbps/1800kbps (up/down) for group hangouts.

▶ Install Google's voice and video chat plug-in. Lesson 11,
    "Chatting on Google+," described the installation of this
    plug-in. If you haven't installed it, however, you can do so at
    www.google.com/chat/video.

NOTE: **Can I Participate in a Hangout from a Mobile Device?**
You can participate in a hangout using an Android 2.3+ mobile
device or an iPhone, iPad, or iPod Touch with iOS 4+. A front-facing
camera is also required. See Lesson 14, "Using Google+ Mobile,"
for more information.

Viewing the Hangouts Page

To get started with Google+ Hangouts, click the **Hangouts** icon on the
Google+ ribbon. Figure 12.1 shows the Hangouts page, which opens.

On this page, you can learn more about hangouts, watch or join an existing
hangout, or start your own hangout.

Starting a Hangout

To start a hangout, follow these steps:

1. On the right side of any Google+ page, click the **Hang Out** but-
    ton, as shown in Figure 12.2.

TIP: **Check Out Other Ways to Hang Out**
You can also start a hangout by clicking the **Hangouts** icon on the
Google+ ribbon and then clicking the **Start a Hangout** button in the
upper-right corner of the Hangouts page. Alternatively, click the **Start**

a Hangout About This Post button at the bottom of any post in the stream. Another option is to go to http://plus.google.com/hangouts to access the Google+ Hangouts page directly from the Web.

FIGURE 12.1   Explore the latest hangouts.

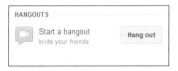

FIGURE 12.2   Hang out with friends on Google+.

2. Click the **Settings** button in the Google+ Hangouts window, as shown in Figure 12.3.

TIP: **Skip Setup If You've Already Used Hangouts**

If you've used Hangouts before and feel confident that your settings are accurate, you can skip steps 3 through 5. If you're new to Hangouts, however, these steps are essential.

Settings button

FIGURE 12.3   Set up Hangouts before using it the first time.

3. In the Settings dialog box, shown in Figure 12.4, verify that your webcam, microphone, and speakers work properly. Optionally, you can select the appropriate camera, microphone, and speakers from the drop-down lists.

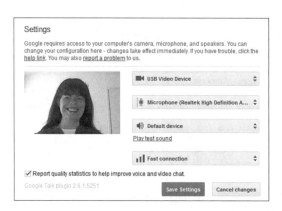

FIGURE 12.4   Verify your settings before starting to hang out.

NOTE: **I'm Having a Setup Problem**

If you're having problems with your webcam or microphone, click the **Help Link** in the Settings dialog box, which opens a page with troubleshooting tips. Common reasons for Hangouts setup problems are not installing the voice and video chat plug-in (www.google.com/chat/video), not turning up your microphone volume, or an outdated webcam driver.

4. Click the **Save Settings** button to save your changes and close the dialog box.

5. Specify who you want to hang out with. Your options include the following:

   ▶ **Everyone in your circles.** By default, Google+ makes your hangout available to everyone in your circles. If you don't want to make this hangout available to this wide an audience, click the **Delete** icon (x) on the right side of the **Your Circles** button.

   ▶ **People in specific circles.** To hang out only with people in a specific circle or circles, click the **Add More People** link. In the menu that opens (see Figure 12.5), select the circle or circles you want to include. For example, you could start a hangout with family members, work friends, and so forth. When you're finished selecting circles, click outside the menu to close it.

   ▶ **A specific person.** This enables you to start a private hangout with another Google+ user. You can click the photo of a person on the right side of the window or type the person's name in the text box and select from the pop-up menu of potential matches (see Figure 12.6).

CAUTION: **Think Carefully About Who You Want to Hang Out With**

Although you can choose to make your hangout available to your extended circles or even the general public, you should think twice before doing so. If someone you don't know or who is disruptive joins a hangout, you can't remove this person without ending the entire hangout. Because only 10 people can participate in a hangout at one time, hangouts are best suited to small group communication.

FIGURE 12.5   You can choose the specific circles and people you want to hang out with.

FIGURE 12.6   You can hang out with just one person.

6. If you want to place calls to landline and mobile phones during your hangout, click the **Telephone** link. Throughout 2012, calls to the United States and Canada are free.

7. Enter a name for your hangout in the Name This Hangout text box. This enables potential participants to know what your hangout is about.

8. Select the **Enable Hangouts on Air** check box if you want to produce a public broadcast. This feature enables you to start a hangout with up to 10 active participants and then choose to let anyone on the Web watch your live broadcast. You can also record Hangouts on Air as YouTube videos for later playback. To learn more, click the question mark next to this check box.

9. If your topic is suited to an adult audience, select the **Restrict Minors from Joining This Hangout** check box.

10. Click the **Hang Out** button to open the Google+ Hangouts window (see Figure 12.7) where you can start your hangout. Be aware that your video feed is now live.

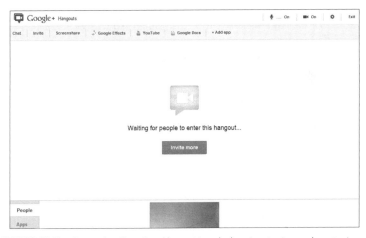

FIGURE 12.7   Open the Google+ Hangouts window to start your hangout.

Google+ alerts the people you chose to hang out with in step 5. As soon as they join, you can start participating in your hangout. See "Joining a Hangout" later in this lesson for more information about how people join a hangout.

NOTE: **My Hangout Isn't Working Properly**

If you're having problems with a hangout, verify that you meet the system requirements specified in "Preparing to Use Hangouts" and that you tested your webcam, microphone, and speakers in step 4. If you did this and are still having problems, try closing any unnecessary programs you have open. If that doesn't work, end your hangout, restart your computer, and start a new hangout.

Inviting People to a Hangout

Once your hangout gets started, you—or anyone in your hangout—can always invite more people. Remember, however, that no matter how many people you invite, Google+ allows only 10 people in a hangout at one time.

To invite people to an in-progress hangout, follow these steps:

1. In the Google+ Hangouts window, click the **Invite More** button (refer to Figure 12.7).

2. Click the **Add Names, Circles, or Email Addresses** link and select the circle or circles you want to invite. Optionally, you can also enter the name of a specific person you want to hang out with.

3. Click the **Invite** button to invite the selected people to the hangout.

Google+ alerts the people you invited to your hangout. See "Joining a Hangout" later in this lesson for more information about how people join a hangout.

Joining a Hangout

Google+ notifies you about hangouts in several ways, each of which enables you to easily join the hangout. When someone in one of your circles is hanging out, Google+:

▶ **Displays a post on your stream.** Click the **Hang Out** button to participate. Figure 12.8 shows a sample post for a hangout.

FIGURE 12.8   Learn about hangouts from your Google+ stream.

▶ **Sends you a notification.** Click the **Notifications** button in the
upper-right corner of any Google+ page, click the right arrow on
a hangout notification, and click the **Hang Out** button to join
(see Figure 12.9).

FIGURE 12.9   Join a hangout with the click of a button.

NOTE: **Google+ Disables Notifications for Large Groups**

If more than 25 people are invited to a hangout (such as the inclu-
sion of a large circle), Google+ won't display a notification. Google+
will alert you to the hangout in your stream, however.

▶ **Displays an invite on the right side of the page.** Click the **Hang Out** button to join.

If someone invites you personally to a hangout (selects your name rather than a circle you belong to), Google+ alerts you about the hangout in the chat window, shown in Figure 12.10. You must be signed in to chat to view this alert. Click the **Join Hangout** button to join the hangout or click the **Ignore** button if you don't want to participate. If the hangout ends, the window closes automatically.

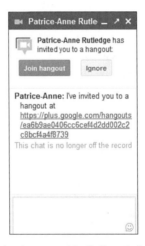

FIGURE 12.10   Learn about personal invitations to hang out in your chat window.

Adding Group Text Chat to a Hangout

You can add text-based chat to your hangout for another way to communicate with your group. Unlike traditional chats, Google+ doesn't retain a record of a chat conducted during a hangout.

To add group text chat to your hangout, follow these steps:

1. Click the **Chat** button in the upper-left corner of the Google+ Hangouts window (refer to Figure 12.7).

2. In the text box at the bottom of the chat window, type your text and press the **Enter** key on your keyboard. Google+ displays your text in the chat window for everyone in the hangout to see, just as it does with a regular chat (see Figure 12.11).

FIGURE 12.11   Participating in group text chat.

3. Participate in group text chat during your hangout.

4. Click the **Chat** button again to close the chat window.

TIP: **Add Some Emotion to Your Group Text Chats**

You can add some emotion to your text with an emoticon, such as a smiley face, sad face, or heart. To do so, click the smiley face icon in the lower-right corner of the chat window. A pop-up box with numerous emoticon possibilities opens, as shown in Figure 12.12. You can select any of these to add a personal touch to your chats. Google+ also converts any text-based emoticon you enter—such as ":-)" to create a smiley face—to a graphic icon in your chat.

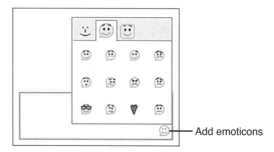

Add emoticons

FIGURE 12.12   Add emotion to your text chat with emoticons such as a smiley face.

Adding Apps to Your Hangouts

To add more interactivity to your hangouts, Google+ enables you to incorporate a variety of applications including YouTube, Google Docs, SlideShare, and others.

Using Screenshare During a Hangout

If you want to discuss something that's on your computer screen during a hangout, you can use the screenshare feature to do so. For example, you could review a presentation or collaborate on a document with a group of people using screenshare.

To use screenshare during your hangout, follow these steps:

1. Click the **Screenshare** button in the upper-left corner of the Google+ Hangouts window (refer to Figure 12.7).

2. In the GoogleTalk Screen Sharing Request dialog box, select the window you want to share.

3. Click the **Share Selected Window** button. The dialog box closes and your shared window displays in your hangout (see Figure 12.13).

4. To stop sharing, click the **Screenshare** button again.

FIGURE 12.13   Select an open window you want to share with people in your hangout.

Adding YouTube Video to Your Hangout

To add more interactivity to your hangouts, Google+ gives you the option of viewing YouTube videos while you're hanging out. Anyone in the hangout can play a YouTube video, not just the person who started the hangout.

To play a YouTube video during your hangout, follow these steps:

1. Click the **YouTube** button at the top of the Google+ Hangouts window (refer to Figure 12.7).

2. Type a search term in the search box in the upper-right corner of the screen and click the **Search** button. For example, you can search for your own videos by entering your name. Optionally, you can play one of the random videos that display in the **Featured Videos** section.

3. Select the video you want to play from the search results, as shown in Figure 12.14.

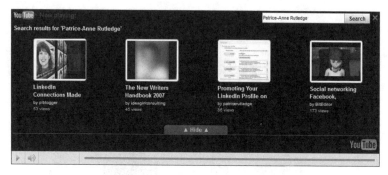

FIGURE 12.14   Select a YouTube video to play in your hangout.

4. Watch the video during your hangout (see Figure 12.15).

FIGURE 12.15   Watching a video during a hangout.

5. By default, Google+ mutes everyone in the hangout while the YouTube video plays. If you want to talk during the video playback, click the **Push to Talk** button. Alternatively, you can click the **Mute** button in the lower-left corner of the YouTube player, which mutes the video soundtrack and unmutes your hangout microphone.

6. Click the **YouTube** button again to close the video.

Applying Google Effects to Your Hangout

To apply special effects during your hangout, click the **Google Effects** button at the top of the Google+ Hangouts window and select an effect from the available options. For example, you can apply humorous effects such as headwear, eyewear, and facial hair. Obviously, these effects aren't suited to every hangout and are most appropriate when you're hanging out just for fun. Click the **Remove All** button to remove all effects. Click the **Close** button (x) to close the Effects pane.

Using Google Docs During a Hangout

To integrate Google Docs with your hangout, click the **Google Docs** button at the top of the Google+ Hangouts window. Using this feature, you can also create shared notes and a shared sketchpad.

Adding Other Apps

To add other applications to your hangout, click the **Add App** button and choose your preferred app. Options include SlideShare (to share SlideShare presentations) or Cacoo for Hangouts (online drawing tool).

Muting During a Hangout

To control sounds and activity during a hangout, you can do the following:

▶ Turn off your microphone by clicking the **On** button (with microphone icon) in the upper-right corner of the Google+ Hangouts window (refer to Figure 12.7). Google+ notifies the other people in your hangout that you're muted by displaying the Mute icon in the upper-right corner of your video thumbnail. For example, if you need to talk to someone else or answer the phone while you're in a hangout, you should mute yourself. You can return to the conversation by clicking the **Off** button, which replaces the On button when you're muted. (It acts as a toggle.)

▶ Mute a loud or boisterous hangout participant by pausing your mouse over this person's video thumbnail and clicking the **Mute** button to the right of this person's name. Be aware, however, that muted participants can unmute themselves at any time.

▶ Turn off your webcam by clicking the **On** button (with video icon) in the upper-right corner of the Google+ Hangouts window (refer to Figure 12.7). Google+ replaces your video thumbnail with a black screen until you click the **Off** button when you're camera-ready again (see Figure 12.16).

FIGURE 12.16   Go black until you're ready to face the camera again.

Ending a Hangout

To end a hangout, click the **Exit** button in the upper-right corner of the Google+ Hangouts window (refer to Figure 12.7).

Summary

In this lesson, you learned how to participate in video chat using Google+ Hangouts. Next, have some fun playing games on Google+.

LESSON 13

Playing Games

In this lesson, you learn how to have fun—and protect your privacy—while playing games on Google+.

Exploring Google+ Games

Google+ offers a variety of online and social games you can play, including Angry Birds, Zynga Poker, Sudoku Puzzles, Edgeworld, Bejeweled Blitz, and other popular games.

To view available games, click the **Games** icon on the Google+ ribbon. If this icon doesn't display on the ribbon, click the **More** icon and select **Games** from the pop-out menu.

On the Games page, you can view featured games as they scroll across your screen (see Figure 13.1).

Playing a Game

Although each game on Google+ has different rules and objectives, the way you access a game is the same for all Google+ games.

To play a game on Google+, follow these steps:

1. Click the **Games** icon on the Google+ ribbon.

2. Click the game you want to play. You can click a game as its preview scrolls across the screen or a game that displays in one of the other sections on the Games page: Play a Game, New Game, or Most Popular (refer to Figure 13.1). Optionally, click the **Directory** button at the top of the page to view a list of all Google+ games that you can filter by category.

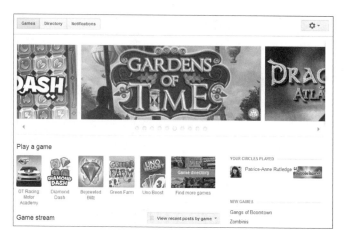

FIGURE 13.1   The Games page previews popular Google+ games.

3. If you've never played a game before, Google+ opens the Games in Google+ Are Social dialog box. Figure 13.2 shows this dialog box, which lets you know how Google+ might share your gaming activity. Click the **Got It, Let's Play** button and then the **Continue** button.

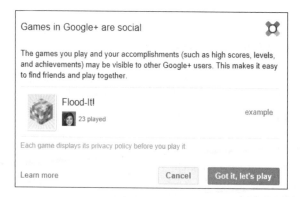

FIGURE 13.2   Google+ informs you that game activity can be public.

NOTE: **What Personal Data Do Games Access and What Do They Do with It?**

The personal data that games access varies by game. For example, a game could view basic information about your account, your email address, a list of people from your circles, and so forth. Google+ games could use this data to display your name and photo as a recent player on the Featured Games page visible to people who have you in circles, or list your name on a game leaderboard within a game.

4. Review what the game wants permission to access and click the **Allow Access** button to go to your game. Most games access your basic account information and the names of people in your circles, but some games access other data as well.

NOTE: **What Happens if I Don't Want to Give Google+ Permission to Access My Data?**

If you click the **No Thanks** button, Google+ doesn't access your data and returns you to the main Games page. Refusing to give permission, however, means that you won't be able to play this game.

Figure 13.3 shows a sample Google+ game, Diamond Dash. Follow the on-screen directions and start playing your game.

After you play a game, it displays in the Your Games section on the Games page. This gives you easy access to the games you enjoy.

When playing games on Google+, you can also do the following:

▶ **Send game invitations and requests**—Many Google+ games allow you to invite friends to play or send other requests to friends. Although the way invitations and requests work vary by game, the process Google+ uses to notify people is the same. Google+ notifies people about your game invitation and they can choose whether to respond.

FIGURE 13.3   Wait until your game loads, and then start playing.

▶ **View and respond to game notifications**—When someone invites you to play a game, sends a game gift, or sends a game-related request, this notification displays on your Game Notifications page. You can access this page by clicking the **Notifications** button at the top of the Games page.

NOTE: **How Do I Remove Game Notifications from the Notifications Menu?**

By default, Google+ displays game-related notifications with other notifications on the Notifications menu (open by clicking the Notifications button in the upper-right corner of any Google+ page). If you don't want to include game notifications, click the **Home** icon on the Google+ ribbon, select **Settings** from the drop-down menu in the upper-right corner of the page, and remove the check mark from the **Show** Google+ Games Notifications in the Google Bar check box (scroll down to find this).

► **Share game activity on the Games stream**—If you're active on Google+ games, you might want to share your gaming success with friends. Using the Games stream, you can publish game updates to those who are interested in such information while not cluttering your main Google+ stream with gaming news. For example, gaming friends might be interested in learning about your highest score ever on Bejeweled Blitz, but those in your Clients and Business Connections circles might not. How you share varies by game, but in general, a game prompts you to click the **Publish** button to share your game results or other game-related news on your Games stream. Remember, however, that sharing is optional. If you don't want to post your game results on the Games stream, don't click the **Publish** button.

TIP: **Consider Creating a Circle for Gaming Friends**

If you play games frequently, consider creating a circle for the friends you play games with. That way, you can more precisely control who you share game updates with and not bother nongaming friends with your news.

► **Buy virtual goods**—Some games on Google+ let you buy virtual goods. For example, you can purchase gold bars on City of Wonder or platinum on Edgeworld. If you decide to spend your hard-earned money on the purchase of virtual goods, you can do so through Google Wallet. Google Wallet enables you to pay for virtual goods using a credit card such as American Express, Visa, MasterCard, or Discover. Although the goods you can buy and their price vary by game, Google+ processes these purchases in a similar way.

► **Remove game permissions**—If you decide you no longer want to play a game or no longer want a game to have access to your personal data, you can remove permissions for that game. To do so, open a game and select **Remove Game** from the drop-down menu in the upper-right corner of the page, as shown in Figure 13.4.

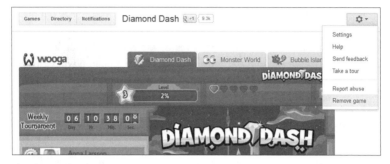

FIGURE 13.4   Remove game permissions if you no longer want a game to access your personal data.

Summary

In this lesson, you learned how to have fun and protect your privacy playing Google+ games. Next, learn how to access Google+ on the go with Google+ Mobile.

LESSON 14

Using Google+ Mobile

In this lesson, you learn how to keep up with Google+ using your mobile phone.

Exploring Google+ Mobile

Google+ Mobile enables you to view selected Google+ data and perform selected Google+ tasks on your mobile phone. Google+ offers four free mobile options:

- ▶ Google+ Android app, for Android 2.2+ users
- ▶ Google+ iPhone app, for iPhone and iPod Touch iOS 4+ users
- ▶ Google+ Mobile web app, for Android 1.5+ users or iPhone and iPod Touch iOS3+ users
- ▶ Google+ Mobile basic web app, for Blackberry 6.0+, Nokia/Symbian, and Windows Mobile users

The available mobile features vary based on which app you use.

Although Google+ Mobile offers much of the same functionality as the web-based version of Google+, it also offers some unique features, such as

- ▶ **Messenger.** Participate in hangouts or group texting, either one-on-one or with the people in one of your Google+ circles. You can invite others or receive a notification on your status bar when someone invites you. With Messenger, you maintain control over who can contact you: anyone on Google+, only people in your circles, or only people in your extended circles. This feature is currently available only for the Google+ Android app and Google+ iPhone app.

▶ **Instant Upload.** Upload photos and videos automatically from your phone to a private Google+ album. You can later make any photos or videos public if you choose to share them. This feature is currently available only for the Google+ Android and iPhone apps. See Lesson 10, "Working with Photos," for more information about Instant Upload.

▶ **Check-ins.** Check into places you visit and view posts from people who are nearby. You must give Google+ permission to share your location to use this feature. Google+ Check-ins is available for the Android app, iPhone app, and Mobile web app.

For detailed instructions on how to use the specific features available for your phone, go to http://support-google.com/plus/?hl=en and click the **Mobile** link.

Using the Google+ Android App

Google+ offers a mobile app for Android users that's available on Google Play at http://play.google.com/store/apps/details?id=com.google.android.apps.plus. This app requires Android 2.2 and later. Figure 14.1 shows the Google+ Android home screen.

The Google+ Android app is a full-featured application that enables you to perform a variety of tasks on your mobile phone. For example, you can

▶ Participate in a group conversation or share photos with Messenger

▶ Start a hangout from Messenger or join an existing hangout

▶ Instantly upload photos to Google+

▶ View and share content on your stream

▶ View profiles

▶ Create and manage circles

▶ Enter and manage comments

- ▶ Post and delete photos

- ▶ View and manage notifications

- ▶ Check into places (if you choose to share your location)

- ▶ View your nearby stream, which displays posts from people who are near you (if you choose to share your location)

FIGURE 14.1   Get mobile access to Google+ from your Android phone.

Using the Google+ iPhone App

Google+ offers a mobile app for iPhone and iPod Touch users that's available on the iTunes App Store at http://itunes.apple.com/us/app/google/id447119634?ls=1&mt=8. This app requires iOS 4 and later. Figure 14.2 shows a sample post with comments on the iPhone.

FIGURE 14.2 Post and comment on Google+ even when you're on the go.

Using the Google+ iPhone app, you can do the following:

▶ Participate in a group conversation or share photos with Messenger

▶ Start a hangout from Messenger or join an existing hangout

▶ Instantly upload photos to Google+

▶ View and share content on your stream

▶ View profiles

▶ Create and manage circles

▶ Enter and manage comments

▶ Post and delete photos

▶ View and manage notifications

▶ Check into places (if you choose to share your location)

▶ View your nearby stream, which displays posts from people who are near you (if you choose to share your location)

Using the Google+ Mobile Web App

The Google+ Mobile web app offers limited mobile functionality for Android 1.5+ users or iPhone and iPod Touch iOS3+ users.

> NOTE: **Why Are There Two Options for Android and iPhone Users?**
>
> The mobile options available to Android, iPhone, and iPod Touch users vary based on the operating system you have. If you have a newer phone (Android 2.2+ or iPhone/iPod Touch iOS 4+), you should use the app designed for your phone rather than the Google+ Mobile web app.

To access the Google+ mobile web app, go to http://google.com/+ on your supported mobile device. Using the web app, you can do the following:

▶ View and share content on your stream

▶ View profiles

▶ Create and manage circles

▶ Enter and manage comments

▶ Check into places (if you choose to share your location)

▶ View your nearby stream, which displays posts from people who are near you (if you choose to share your location)

Using the Google+ Mobile Basic Web App

The Google+ Mobile basic web app offers limited mobile functionality for Blackberry 6.0+, Nokia/Symbian, and Windows Mobile users.

To access the basic web app, go to http://google.com/+ on your supported mobile device. Using the basic web app, you can view and share content on your stream. If you choose to share your location, you can also view your nearby stream, which displays posts from people who are near you.

Summary

In this lesson, you learned how to access Google+ from your mobile phone and download device-specific mobile apps for the Android, iPhone, and iPod Touch, as well as for Blackberry, Nokia/Symbian, and Windows Mobile users.

Index

Symbols

+1, enabling on non-Google sites, 78
+1 button, 4-5
    liking posts, 114-115
+1 personalization, enabling, 86-105
+1's tab, 36
2-step verification, 77

A

About tab, editing, 27-30
abuse, reporting, 126-127
accessing
    Google+ features, 14
    streams, 110
Account, 15
account settings, managing, 75-78
Accounts page, privacy, 75
acquaintances, 58
Add Account, 15

adding
    apps to hangouts, 189-191
    circles to pages, 48
    cover photos to profiles, 21
    Google effects to hangout, 191
    Google+ profile button to
        websites, 40
    group text chat to hangouts,
        186-188
    links to profiles, 32-34
    managers to pages, 52-53
    pages to circles, 87
    people to circles, 60-61
        from email contacts, 63-66
        *from Find People tab,
            61-62*
        *from Notifications menu,
            66-68*
        from profiles, 68-69
        with suggestions, 66-2001
    photo scrapbooks to profiles,
        23-24

photos
> to existing photo albums,
> 153-154
> to pages, 45
> to profiles, 8

single cover photos to profiles,
21-22

YouTube video to hangout,
189-190

albums, creating, 101

alternate email addresses, 78

approving tags, 158-161

apps, adding to hangouts, 189-191

availability, chat list, 164-165

B

backing up data, 89-91

blocking people, 124

bragging rights, 28

buying virtual goods in games, 197

C

Change Password link, 76

Change Recovery Options link, 77

chat
> off the record, 174-176
> participating in, 166-168
> privacy settings, 166
> sending files, 169-170
> signing out of, 176
> video chat, 170 172, 174

participating in, 170-174
> voice chat, 170-173
> > participating in, 173-174

chat list, 163-164
> availability, 164-165
> color-coded icons, 164

check-ins, Google+ Mobile, 200

circles, 4, 57-58
> adding people to
> > from email contacts, 63-66
> > from Find People tab,
> > 61-62
> > people to, 60-61
> > from profiles, 68-69
> > with suggestions, 66

> from Notifications menu, 66-68
> > adding to pages, 48, 87
> > creating, 59-60
> > deleting, 72
> > editing names and
> > descriptions, 71-72
> > Extended Circles, 63
> > moving people from one
> > circle to another, 70
> > removing people, 71
> > sharing, 72-74
> > viewing
> > > people in your
> > > circles, 69
> > > people who added you to
> > > their circles, 69-70

color-coded icons, chat list, 164

commenting on posts, 116

comments
> deleting, 117, 124
> disabling, 122
> editing, 116-117
> reporting, 123-124

connecting pages to websites, 48

contact settings, profiles, 36-37

content, searching, 131-133

Contributor To, profiles, 30

Creative Kit, editing photos, 161-162

D

data, backing up, 89-91

deleting

circles, 72

comments, 117, 124

Google accounts, 79-80

pages, 51-52

people from Find People tab, 63

photo albums, 152-153

photos from profiles, 25-26

posts, 122

profiles, 78-79

disabling comments, 122

displaying

content about games, 87

posts in real-time, 133

E

Edit Profile link, 76

editing

About tab, 27-30

circles, names and descriptions, 71-72

comments, 116-117

names in profiles, 26-27

photos, Creative Kit, 161-162

posts, 121

education, profiles, 29

email, receiving notifications, 140-141

email contacts, adding people to circles, 63-66

from exported files, 65-66

email subscriptions

managing, 85

pages, 50

employment, profiles, 28-29

ending hangouts, 192

Explore page, viewing, 128

Extended Circles, 63

F

family, 57

feedback, sending, 16-17

files, sending during chat, 169-170

filtering

search results, 133

streams, 113-114

Find People tab

adding people to circles, 61-62

deleting people, 63

following, 58

formatting posts, 98

friends, 57

G

games, 193-194
  buying virtual goods, 197
  displaying content about
    games, 87
  invitations, 195
  notifications, 196
  personal data, 195
  playing, 193-198
  removing permissions, 197
  sharing on Games stream, 197
Games page, 193-194
Games stream, sharing game
  activity, 197
Gender, profiles, 30
Google accounts, deleting, 79-80
Google docs, 191
Google effects, adding, 191
Google+, 3
  navigating, 13-14
  signing in to, 12-13
  signing up for, 5-12
  using as a page, 48-49
Google+ Android app, 200-201
Google+ features, accessing, 14
Google+ iPhone app, 201-202
Google+ Mobile, 199-200
  basic web app, 203
  Google+ Android app, 200-201
  Google+ iPhone app, 201-202
Google+ Mobile web app, 203
Google+ page, 42-48
Google+ Mobile basic web app, 203
Google+ Mobile web app, 203

Google+ profile button, adding to
  websites, 40
Google+ Ripples, 120
Google+ suggestions, 62-63
group text chat, adding to hangouts,
  186-188

H

hangouts, 5, 177
  adding
    apps to, 189-191
    group text chat to, 186-188
  ending, 192
  inviting people to, 184
  joining, 184-186
  muting, 191-192
  preparing to use, 177-178
  screenshare, 188
  starting, 178-184
Hangouts page, viewing, 178
help, 15-16
Home, profiles, 29
Hotmail, adding contacts to
  circles, 64

I

Instant Upload, 5, 200
  Google+ Mobile, 200
introductions, 28
invitations
  for games, 195
  signing up for Google+, 7
inviting people to hangouts, 184

J-K

joining hangouts, 184-186

L

languages, specifying preferred, 88-89

lightbox, 155-156

lightbox view, removing tags, 159

liking posts with +1 button, 114-115

linking to posts, 125

links

adding to profiles, 32-34

sharing, 105-107

locking posts, 123

Looking For, profiles, 30

M

managers

adding to pages, 52-53

removing from pages, 53-54

managing

account settings, 75-78

photo settings, 87

on pages, 51

privacy settings, 82-83

for profiles, 81

for sharing, 81-82

products, 87

security, 79-80

settings, 49-52, 83-84

+1 personalization, 86

adding pages to circles, 87

displaying content about games, 87

email subscriptions, 50, 84

photo settings, 87

setting notification delivery preferences, 50, 84

specifying notification delivery preferences, 50, 85-86

specifying who can interact with you and your posts, 50, 84

mentioning other people, posts, 99

messenger, 5

Messenger, Google+ Mobile, 199

moving people from one circle to another, 70

multiple sign-in, 78

muting

hangouts, 191-192

posts, 127-128

N

names, editing in profiles, 26-27

navigating Google+, 13-14

notification delivery preferences

settings, 84-85

specifying, 50

notification preferences

pages, 50-51

specifying, 85-86

Notifications, 14-15

notifications, 135
    games, 196
    receiving via email and text
        message, 140-141
    specifying who can send to
        you, 141
    viewing, 136-139
Notifications menu, adding people to
    circles, 66-68
Notifications page, viewing, 139-140

O

occupation, 28
off the record, chat, 174-175
organizing photo albums, 151-152
Other Names, profiles, 30
Other Profiles, 30

P

pages, 4, 48-49
    adding managers, 52-53
    circles, adding, 48
    connecting to websites, 48
    creating, 42-48
    deleting, 51-52
    email subscriptions, 50
    notification preferences, 50-51
    photo settings, managing, 51
    photos, adding, 45
    versus profiles, 41-42
    removing managers, 53-54
    settings, 49-50

specifying notification delivery
    preferences, 50
specifying who can interact
    with you and your posts, 50
transferring ownership of
    pages, 54
participating
    in chat, 166-168
    in video chat, 174
in voice chat, 173-174
people
    adding to circles, 60-61
        from email contacts, 63-66
        from Find People tab,
        61-62
        from Notifications menu,
        66-68
        from profiles, 68-69
        with suggestions, 66-2001
    blocking, 124
    deleting from Find People
        tab, 63
    inviting to hangouts, 184
    moving from one circle to
        another, 70
    removing from circles, 71
    specifying who to display on
        profiles, 37-39
    viewing
        those who added you to
        their circles, 69-70
        in your circles, 69
permissions, removing game
    permissions, 197
personal data, games, 195

phones, uploading photos, 102

photo albums, 145

  adding photos to existing albums, 153-154

  creating, 146-147

  deleting, 152-153

  organizing, 151-152

  sharing, 148-150

  updating sharing settings, 150-151

  viewing, 147-148

photo lightbox, 154-155

photo options, 143

photo scrapbooks, adding to profiles, 23-24

photo settings

  managing, 87

  pages, managing, 51

photos, 155-156

  adding

    to existing photo albums, 153-154

    to pages, 45

    to profiles, 8, 21

  albums, creating, 101

  deleting from profiles, 25-26

  editing with Creative Kit, 161-162

  sharing, 100-102

  single cover photos, adding to profiles, 21-22

  tagging, 156-157

  uploading, 143-144

    from phones, 102

Photos page, 144-145

Photos tab, 35

Picasa Web Albums, 143

Places Lived, profiles, 29

playing games, 193-198

posts, 120-121

  commenting on, 116

  comments

    deleting, 124

    reporting, 123-124

  deleting, 122

  disabling comments, 122

  displaying in real-time, 133

  editing, 121

  formatting, 98

  liking with +1 button, 114-115

  linking to, 125

  locking, 123

  mentioning other people, 99

  muting, 127-128

  reporting abuse, 126-127

  sharing, 93-97, 117-120

  viewing

    Explore page, 128

    streams, 110-113

Posts tab, 35

preferred languages, specifying, 88-89

Privacy, 15

privacy, 75

  managing account settings, 75-78

  profiles, specifying, 30-32

privacy settings
    chat, 166
    managing, 82-83
        for profiles, 81
        for sharing, 81-82
products, managing, 87-88
Profile Discovery, profiles, 30
profiles, 3-4, 19-21
    About tab, editing, 27-30
    adding
        cover photos, 21
        links, 32-34
        people to circles, 68-69
        photo scrapbooks, 23-24
        photos, 8
single cover photos, 21-22
    contact settings, 36-37
    deleting, 78-79
    names, editing, 26-27
    versus pages, 41-42
    people, specifying who to
        display, 37-39
    photos, deleting, 25-26
    privacy, specifying, 30-32
    privacy settings, 81
    tabs, specifying, 34-36
    viewing as others see it, 39

R

receiving notifications via email and
    text message, 140-141
Recommended Links, profiles, 30-39
relationships, profiles, 30

removing
    game permissions, 197
    managers from pages, 53-54
    people from circles, 71
    tags, 158-159
reporting
    abuse, 126-127
    comments, 123-124
Ripples, 120

S

saving searches, 133
screenshare, hangouts, 188
search results, filtering, 133
searches, saving, 133
searching content, 131-133
security, managing, 79-80
sending
    feedback, 16-17
    files during chat, 169-170
settings, managing, 83-84
    +1 personalization, 86
    adding pages to circles, 87
    displaying content about
        games, 87
    email subscriptions, 85
    photo settings, 87
    setting notification delivery
        preferences, 84-85
    specifying notification delivery
        preferences, 85-86
    specifying who can interact
        with you and your posts, 84

Share, 15
share box, 93-98
sharing
 circles, 72-74
 game activity, on Games
  stream, 197
 links, 105-107
 photo albums, 148-150
  updating settings, 150-151
 photos, 100-102
 posts, 93-97, 117-120
 privacy settings, 81-82
 with share box, 93-98
 videos, 103-104
signing in
 to Google+, 12-13
 multiple sign-in, 78
signing out, 15
 of chat, 176
signing up for Google+, 5-12
starting hangouts, 178-184
streams, 4, 12, 109
 accessing, 110
 filtering, 113-114
 posts, 120-121
  commenting on, 116
  deleting, 122
  deleting comments, 124
  disabling comments, 122
  editing, 121
  liking with +1 button,
   114-115
  linking to, 125
  locking, 123

  muting, 127-128
  reporting abuse, 126-127
  reporting comments,
   123-124
  sharing, 117-120
  viewing Explore page, 128
  viewing posts, 110-113
  What's Hot stream, 128
 suggestions, 62-63
  adding people to circles, 66

T

tabs, displaying on profiles, 34-36
tagging photos, 156-157
taglines, 28
tags
 approving, 158-161
 removing, 158-159
text messages, notifications,
 receiving, 140-141
transferring ownership of pages, 54

U

updating album sharing settings,
 150-151
uploading
 photos, 143-144
  from phones, 102
 videos, 103

V

video chat, 170-173
    participating in, 174
videos
    adding, 189-190
    sharing, 103-104
    uploading, 103
Videos tab, 35
View Profile, 15
viewing
    Explore page, 128
    Hangouts page, 177-178
    moving people from one circle
        to another, 69-70
    notifications, 136-139
    Notifications page, 139-140
    people in your circles, 69
    photo albums, 147-148
    posts, streams, 110-113
    profile, 39
virtual goods, buying in games, 197
voice chat, 170-173
    participating in, 173-174

W

websites
    adding Google+ profile button,
       40
    connecting to pages, 48
What's Hot stream, 128
work, profiles, 29

X-Y-Z

Yahoo! Mail, adding contacts to
    circles, 64-65
YouTube
    adding video, 189-190
    uploading photos, 104

Try Safari Books Online FREE for 15 days
Get online access to Thousands of Books and Videos

Safari Books Online
FREE 15-DAY TRIAL + 15% OFF*
informit.com/safaritrial